AF553778

MANAGEMENT INFORMATION SYSTEM

MANAGEMENT INFORMATION SYSTEM

DR. B. NARAYAN

A.P.H. PUBLISHING CORPORATION
7, ANSARI ROAD, DARYA GANJ
NEW DELHI - 110 002

Published by

S. B. Nangia
A.P.H. Publishing Corporation
7, Ansari Road, Darya Ganj
New Delhi-110002

2022

Typeset at
NEW APCON
25/2, Panchsheel Shopping Centre
New Delhi 110 017
☎ 6490802

Printed in India at
Efficient Offset Printers
New Delhi-110 035

CONTENTS

PREFACE

Managers and supervisors clamor for current information and guidelines to help solve formidable problems in their work world—problems that range from "how to do it" to "how to resolve conflict when doing it." Many problems are generated from miscommunication and incompetence. Managers and supervisors cannot wait for research breakthroughs with real-world answers to solve these dilemmas. Whether making a decision, solving a problem setting up a procedure, designing a process, or resolving a behaviour conflict, a manager must rely heavily on information. To a great extent, management practitioners are information workers; that is, they generate, distribute, store, retrieve, and consume information.

This book, sets the stage for introducing the interplay of information systems with the world of business and how increasingly information systems are becoming critical corporate resource is highlighted. Information, for the modern organisation, is a resource parallel in importance to land, labour, and capital.

In this book, there are seemingly infinite number of definitions for this term, both in a data processing context and in common usage. Information is meaning assigned to data. For the purpose of any system or organisation, information is data that have been processed into a form that is meaningful to the recipient or user and is of real or perceived value in current or prospective decision processes.

This book should be of great help to managerial practitioners at any organizational level who are responsible for a function, department, or set of responsibilities. This book will also give these practitioners insights into management roles and approaches in other areas as well. Students of management in university or educational institutions will find the series an invaluable resource for adding "real world" practices to their academic and theoretical foundations.

Editors

1

FUNDAMENTALS OF MANAGEMENT INFORMATION SYSTEMS

This chapter introduces you to five fundamental types of information systems. Transaction Processing Systems (TPS) support the operational, day-to-day activities of the organization. Management information systems are used to facilitate the management of those day-to-day activities. Decision Support Systems (DSS) are special-purpose applications that exist to support the resolution of particular problems or make decisions to take advantage of unique opportunities. Office Automation Systems (OAS) facilitate office activities such as the preparation and communication of correspondence. Finally, Executive Support Systems (ESS) are systems employed by very senior managers to keep abreast of the organization in broad, overview terms.

In this section we will try to explain the interconnection that exists between management organisation and its processes, and MIS. For obvious reasons, the coverage will be highly condensed and will bring out only salient points.

Genesis

Ever since man realised that a co-operative society was

necessary to achieve his goals, some form of "managing" was an inescapable result, paralleling economic development and value systems. This is best achieved by structuring organisations to solve problems efficiently. The new class of workers, called managers, evolved with some distinct functions;

— to perform the structuring i.e. form organization;

— to influence individuals and groups to cooperate and achieve objectives;

The Industrial Revolution led to larger organisations, and formalised information systems (abbreviated to infosys in future) made their entry to meet decision-making needs. This MIS is on the basis of management tasks; management principles; style of individuals and organisation structure and behaviour.

Organisational theory

Organisation and Management theories differ in two ways: organisation is the structure of interpersonal relations and it is a mechanism for promoting collaboration with management. Organisation can be seen as the vehicle to achieve objectives. Moreover, organisation theory is relatively new.

There are various models existing under the organisation theory. These are: Decision-making; Bureaucracy Social Systems and Systems Models.

— Herbert Simon propounded the 'Decision-making Approach': organisation members were according to him decision makers and problems solvers are concluded that "Administration processes are decisional processes";

— Max Weber propounded the Bureaucracy model; in

which there is delineation of the structural and procedural characteristics of the Bureaucracy, the hierarchial structure of authority and notion of discipline based on formal position. These concepts are still valid.

— Talcott Parsons, a major proponent, looked at organisations as social systems, which came up consequent to the complexities of modern societies, with primary of orientation to a goal.

— Behavioural theories have led to the modern organisation and management theories.

A quick look will now be taken at the various theories that have contributed to what has come to be best suited to the modern manager.

Classical process theory

Basic tenets, credited to Henri Fayol, Fredrick W. Taylor, L. Guick and Lyndall Urwick and J.D. Mooney are:

— Clear lines of authority i.e. chain of command to the Chief Executive

— Specialisation of labour in groups to increase productivity leading to the concept of departments;

— Unity of command i.e. reporting to one person only;

— Span of control to be limited, by nature of task;

— Clear division of line and staff functions; staff to be advisers with no charter to influence;

The acronym POSDCORB is coined for the process of managing meaning planning, Organising, Staffing, Directing, Coordinating, Reporting and Budgeting by Moony. Basic premise of classical school is that organising is a logical, rational process; with a clear objective where "units" are involved in some specific "work" and the position of these units are defined in terms of accountability. The organisations charts emerge and the position description of duties is thus well defined.

The Classical theory is valuable and widely followed. It is however limited by its concentration on the formal anatomy and structure and its insistence that human problems will take care of themselves; once tasks are assigned and duties organised. It overlooks human interaction and behaviour patterns in any organised groups.

Behavioural theory

The Hawthorne experiments found that employee morale is more important to productivity than technical or physical environment. This led to research on leadership and motivation. A motivated work force is a *sine qua* non for the productivity. Social scientists under this theory believe that all people are not equal, they are being influenced by many factors—physical, mental, background of experience, perception of situation, critical faculties and even, with age. You have studied the various motivation theories namely (i) Maslow's need hierarchy theory (ii) Herzberg's two factor theory (iii) Vroom's model etc., in detail in companion volumes of this text. These theories are therefore not repeated here. You are expected to know the basic concepts and main points under each. Differences apart (between the approach of all motivation theories), the common message to managers is: determine what each worker wants, construct tasks and create conducive environment for goal achievement; develop an incentive/reward system.

Group dynamics

Kurt Lewin used this term to designate forces and behaviour that occur within the group (people group together to satisfy needs of affiliation, security, identity and power). The informal organisation refers to the total of member-initiated institutions that exists without formal sanction. The formal and informal orgs modify, supplement and reinforce or weaken each other. Six types of informal groups may be identified: the total organisation (all the many interlocking groups/sub-systems in the entire organisation); union vs non-union etc.); Primary cliques (people with similar jobs or common interests e.g. maintenance crew; top executives who cliques (people with similar jobs or common interests e.g. maintenance crew; top executives who Work and eat together in the executive dining hall); cliques (any small group aiming for power or social advantage); friendship/ kinship group (close to social/neighbourhood/family ties e.g. north Indians in the south Indian companies) isolates (the odd men, loners etc).

Determinants for informal groups: (i) location (physical location in plant or office); (ii) occupation (similar taste/ interests e.g. music) (iii) special issues (on a common cause; the group normally disbands after issue is over).

Informal organisation: An informal organisation will always exist in all organisations. In designing MISs, its existence must be accepted and allowed for.

Some characteristics of informal organisation are: (i) they act as agents of social control; (ii) they are examples of human interaction (quite different and hence analysis has to be quite different from those of formal organisation); (iii) status and communications systems exist divorced from the formal structure; (iv) resist change of any form; (v) informal leader (who is not necessarily the formally appointed one).

Communication: It is one of the primary roles of the informal organisation. Employees communi-cate laterally and vertically to get jobs done; often when official channels fail to give full or correct information. Communication through this informal channel travels fast. This is called "Grapevine" when an official information is leaked through this channel.

Conformity: It is one of the characteristics of the informal organisation exercised through social control. Group norms cannot be easily changed by management except by canvassing the aid of influential members. Group discipline can be very sever.

Power and authority: Authority, loosely, could mean 'legitimate' right to command and apply sanctions and hence is conferred by the formal organisation.

The source of authority is explained in many ways: (i) institutional (derived from accepted cultural institutions—traditional, legal or theological); (ii) subordinate (managers have authority to the degree that subordinates accept decisions; thus authority flows from bottom up and is gained by leadership); (iii) organisational relationship (by virtue of authority of the position); (iv) legal decree (in Govt.); (v) personal acceptance or consultative (by recognition of the leader by popularity, past achievements, integrity, professionalism, skill/knowledge). (vi) Charismatic which is often based on irrational faith); (vii) identification (belongingness consequent to strong association with the group; (viii) sanctions (power to reward or punish); (ix) authority of the situation (integrates the goal of the organisation and the individuals involved. Authority does not leap forth from the command of those at the top but arises out of the law of the situation—the manager and subordinates get together, discuss alternative, arrive are course of action called for by the "situation". Direct application of authority may lead to rebellion, reluctant acceptance, eager participation or habitual acceptance depending on the culture of the organisation.

Power and authority does no leap form the command of those at the top by arises out of the law of the situation—the manager and subordinates get together, discuss alternatives, arrive at the course of action called for by the "situation". Direct application of authority may lead to rebellion, reluctant acceptance, eager participation or habitual acceptance depending on going culture of the organisation.

Power and authority are considered separate entities by many writers. Authority is delinked from power when a group willingly accepts leadership of persons.

Cooperation in an organisation is a strong need for individuals with affiliation and stability. For those who covertly seek power, cooperation is forced by mutual goals. The view that conflict is harmful to goals is no longer true; the modern view is that there is much constructive potential in conflict; deliberate" controlled competition" is often advised. Other than integration and cooperation, solutions to conflict are: victory/defeat; compromise; avoidance of subject and deadlock. MIS creators should be aware of these aspects and handle the situation in a correct perspective.

Leadership: For effective and efficient management of resources, leaders should be aware of some behaviour patterns to lead. They should provide values and focus on action, so that they influence others to act. Leaders play a different role *vis-a-vis* followers and must have some typical characteristics. Leadership may be official (through organisation position); informal (personal attributes); formal (one who commands both positional and personal influence). The last should be the profile of a manager.

Leadership style: Keith Davis defined four leadership styles in the environment of the theory that it varies in a continuum from task oriented to person oriented. These are autocratic, custodial, supportive and collegial. The middle two conform to Herzberg's positive motivators. It should be apparent that leaders cannot be both task and person oriented; further, task achievement will be high if people orientation is high (the book, "In Search of Excellence" highlights this as the single reason for success of the selected companies in Fortune's first hundred). Of course organisational goals and workers goals are supportive but the degree of effectiveness depends on their divergence as the lower. According to Robert R. Blake and Jane S Mouton "goals of the organisation and needs of workers are not incompatible" and have projected a managerial grid of rating.

The behaviour approaches have gradually led to the "situational approach". Fred Fiedler's leader effectiveness curve, is a condensed version showing that at the most favourable and most unfavourable situation, he is not effective if he is task oriented but is rated very low as a co-worker by his group.

The behaviour approaches have gradually led to the "situational approach". Fred Fielder's leader effectiveness curve, is a condensed version showing that at the most favourable and most unfavourable situation, he is not effective if he is task oriented but is rated very low as a co-worker by his group.

Decision theory: Simon equated managing to decision-making and processes leading to its as the prime task of managers. Pre-decision activities are finding occasions, finding possible courses and choosing a course. It is the nuclues of the systems approach but it would be a good policy to accept other approaches as contributing to the totality of knowledge of his/her requirement to manage; it is to be borne in perspective that decision neither commences an action nor completes it.

Systems theory of organisation and management: Synthesising the functions of management and separate approaches to the study of organisation and management, a SYSTEM of organisation and management emerges. To build a conceptual model to manage the transformation of resource flows through the organisation by means of a systems approach is the task.

The Systems Approach is "a system that integrates the parts: resource flows through the organisation by means of a systems approach is the task.

The Systems Approach is "a system that integrates the parts: resource flows, functions of management, organisation theory and the various techniques". The new component which we are to study—a Management Information System, provides information for planning, activates plans and furnishes the essential feed back to achieve stability through control.

The organisation and MIS

Unless the behaviour of the organisation's people is considered, design of best MISs will fail even though technically it may be sound. The key factors to be considered are: social organisations with its norms, roles, relationships and communications, networks; psychological needs of esteem, self-actualisation and freedom from repressive control.

Resistance to change

MIS introduction is a threat to an individual in organisation relationships and psychological needs. Management must do more than involving all in MIS development, particularly the new patterns in organisation structure which will develop as a result of introduction of MIS etc. Resistance must be avoided rather than defeated by sheer power.

It is the social change that will be resisted, not the technological change. The newly required behavioural patterns, translating inputs to outputs, may cause heavals, by mismatch. This dictates modification of the organisation pattern on positive potential, so that people see MIS features as supportive to their social and psychological needs.

Commonly met resistance factors are:

— Isolation-being dependent on the computer, deprived of "personal" data; loss of importance

— Superior-subordinate relations change; revised information flow;

— Job ambiguity and loss of control—since "decisions" are "taken" by the computer;

— Time rigidity information as an assembly line needs timely action;

— Interpersonal relationship change informal groups get broken.

Change sans resistance

To bring about change without resistance the following may be of help:

(a) Create climate for change: Show the weaknesses in existing system by org-wide seminars' meetings and workshops and build up urge for change.

(b) Develop effective agents of change: Select carefully, informal leaders of stature and win support by extramural workshops, seminars and so on. Simulated thus, incorporating them in MIS teams would benefit not only in getting support of those groups but also, more importantly, get worker desires incorporated.

(c) Modify "required" organisation: It is required to fit the technical side but this may need to be modified to meet working relationships. Adjustment of technical as well as working relationships must be there in an organisation. As introduction of MIS may disturb this, the new organisation should be modified to take care of working relationship besides the technical ones.

Management, information and the systems approach

Systems approach is eclectic, absorbing all new models, concepts, approaches, validated principles etc.

Tasks and functions of management according to this approach are:

— match capabilities to environment needs and missions.

— establish a work environment and allocation of resources for maximum productivity of the total (organisational) system;

— manage responsibilities, POSDCORB functions. Staffing is behaviourally related to organising; initiating (directing) is behaviour oriented.

We will now focus on planning, organising and controlling from systems and information perspectives.

The general management system

The three functions, planning, organising, and controlling, mutually impinge on each other, in the management process. This figure shows the function of planning, organising, directing, controlling and feedback.

The management process is iterative. An adequate management system would be the function for the MIS to succeed, including organisational arrangement, structure and procedures for planning and control, clear objectives and all other manifestations of good organisation and management.

The Management System: develops plans to achieve objective;

organises for implementation of plans;

control performances so that schedules of plans and action are met

Planning: Deciding in advance, what has to be done, who has to do it, when it has to be done and how it has to be done; bridging the gap from where we are to where we want to go. All managers do it, to plan allocation resources and work to other people.

Planning is important due to:

— realisation to be prepared for events to react to them;

— growth in competition;

— CBIs growth with computer power going up and costs going down;

— increased complexity of modern business as also high risk heavy investment;

— advances of planning theory.

Dimensions of plans

Plans are followed by policies to give direction to the plans. Policies are of two types: Those that limit discretionary actions and those that specify procedures.

Strategic plans: Provide the framework for the systems approach to planning. It is not detailed, since current environments (like competition) would determine parameters. But the long-term goals would set the constrain for the medium and short range goals. The strategic plan ties up the development plan, which focuses on the short range growth through internal or external expansion. The operation plan (usually of one year) are then made.

Strategic planning is two-phased; (i) developing a strategy; (ii) formulating the milestones, time cost etc. (referred to as strategic/long-term plan). Strategy is the profile at a future data and is made up of: scope, competitive edge, target specifications and resource assignment.

Strategic planning process consists of analysing environment (including new opportunities), identifying company's strengths/weaknesses, taking top management views, assessing threats/opportunities, defining product/ market scope, defining edge over others, establishing objectives and measures of performance and defining resource development.

Short range planning. It is usually finance biased, objectives and standards of performance being so defined. Profit centres are established with turnover, sales etc defined, leading to measurable and controllable elements like investments (fixed assets, inventory etc.) and cost of sales (direct labour, transportation etc.)

Information and planning. Planning Information are of three types: environmental, competitive, and internal.

Organising. Consists of grouping of tasks to accomplish plans. Good job descriptions, roles etc must be unambiguous for a good organising to take place.

Systems approach to organising. The interactive approach is the best. The phases here would be: chalk out an organisation; develop a classical hierarchy to meet objectives; develop a balanced organisation based on analysis of decision (could be matrix, team or system type).

The classical hierarchical structure is the best concept as a foundation to variations later.

Structure is the key word and departmentation is the corollary. Examples are: Functional (selling, finance etc.), product, territory, customer (banking, Govt. etc.), process etc, Matrix, team/task force and four dimensional (cost centres, business profit centres, international profit centres and time) are variations.

Information and organising. Can be seen as analogous to the human anatomy (structure) and the nervous system (info), Information must conform to the organisation structure and delegation. Mismatch between them may be due to lag of information to support organisation changes. As needs, structure and managers change, information must; else there will be "Information Lag".

Controlling. Ideally, plans will be flawlessly executed by a perfectly balanced organisation; this is rare, and therefore control must exist.

Generally, it is a three stage process: (1) Set standards of performance. It may be quantitative for example, a 10% increase in sales-or-qualitative like maintain high morale; (ii) Measure performance (oral or written after personal observation) lastly, (iii) Correcting deviation.

MIS: The manager's view

Dreamt of, in the 60s, as an essential ingredient to the Systems Approach to Management, MIS somehow fell out of favour in the 70s; particularly since managers saw it as an attempt to design a monolithic system to encompass the entire operations of a company, in total. Such a concept (even if computer persons did not spell it out in so many words) was difficult to swallow for the enlightened Manager, who wondered how computer could quantify the information that he knows is subjective and psychological in nature and is often as important as the quantitative type.

The lack of coherent thinking on the part of the specialists led to MIS meaning as simple a thing as payroll to complicated modelling for complex situation. Despite this, where there had been a good rapport between the data processing (DP) personnal and Management, some very good MIS was developed on a planned basis.

MIS is not necessarily computer based but current usage and the rapid development in technology has resulted in MIS being connotative with Computer Based Information Systems (CBIS). Some writers recommend the use of the term Information Resource Management (IRM) since Information has come to be seen as a corporate resource, as important as cash. Interestingly, writers have seen the "organisation replacing "cash" with "information" as the prime resource to be managed.

The Genesis

The 60s saw management sciences opening the exciting portals of the "Systems Approach"; and the emergence of the term "Management Information Systems (MIS)" that is probably the *most* ill used term in centuries. As Kanter put it, it provided the "wish-fulfilment syndrome" which he saw developing this way:

— When one had a serious problem and an approach emerges that, although only partially understood, appears to bear some relation to the problem, this approach tends to become the solution;

— The next phase is the "nonfulfilment backlash"; disenchantment, disillusionment, disappointment followed in the ranks of managers and professionals.

In retrospect, organisations did not have the tools that are commonplace today. MIS properly defined, and understood, is a gold mine; it is the only way to meet the growing demand for information.

To start with, we should be clear as to what it is not: it is not the "inventory status report" or the "payroll"; it is not the books on "MIS" solely describing input, output and processing characteristics of computers that present "MIS" in its true form.

A great disservice has been the professional trying to

build "Total Systems" doomed to failure from the word "go"; such grandiose efforts are the gibbets on which "MIs" hang in shame. Managers have learnt that it cannot quantify information that is subjective and psychological in nature; it is as important as the quantitative type. They have also learnt that it cannot assist all levels by the simple process of "press-a-button".

Anatomy of MIS

The simplest definition of MIS is "a system that aids management in making, implementing and controlling decisions".

Analysing the statement,

— Decision-making, including the pre-processes, can be termed planning;

— Management can be defined (without prejudice to classical ones like getting things done through people) as the planning and control of resources, like people, to achieve objectives.

MIS is made up of three basic ingredients: Management, Information and System. The first is a vast subject in itself; the second is given as Chapter System is covered later in this chapter.

Although Management is a subject that takes many semesters to cover, some salient parts are covered in this section and explained in previous section.

Levels of management

Although no clear lines of demarcation exist, in a typical organisation we may have multiple layers upto either. But assuming that three levels is a *sine qua non*, we may find almost all organisations have the following interactions:

— Top Management establishes policies, plans and objectives as also the framework of a budget; passed downwards.

— Middle Management converts has specific schedules and measurement yardsticks.

Planning: Organisations generally go in for a three-tiered planning process: a long term, typically five years; a medium range, typically two years; and a current plan, typically one year. The MIS would be an integral part helping, as it will, in formulation, monitoring and control.

System is the third ingredient of MIS, and defined as " a set or arrangement of things so related or connected to form a unity or organisation". Using the "black box" concept, a system consists of an input to the box and an output from it; a system normally has a feed back element for control of the system to operate as per the objectives set for it. Where it differs from business systems is that it is composed of both a physical and information sub-systems. It can be viewed as being built up of a number of information sub-systems to support various processes.

Characteristics

Although MIS is a difficult concept to place in a succinct, condensed form, certain characteristics need to be mentioned if not elaborated upon: it is management oriented; it is management directed; it is integrated; there are common data flows; there is a heavy planning element; there is a sub-system concept; it should be flexible and easy to use; data bases are implicit; there is a move to distributed data processing. Overriding all this is the realisation that data is a corporate resource.

These certain characteristics are discussed below:-

(1) Management oriented: Whether on a top down or bottom up philosophy, MIS is oriented to management need. However, equally, the system will bear in mind the corporate aims and objectives.

(2) Management directed: Involvement is tantamount to lip service to MIS; active direction is necessary. In a good MIS environment, managers would be spending a good deal of time in system analysis/design. Far from being a one time effort, this continuity will be maintained during the system life cycles i.e. in the review and redesign. It is only then that trade-off decisions between alternatives can be realistic. It is in this regard that a steering committee is almost mandatory.

(3) Integrated: The term is not used in the context of a "total systems" approach where every information system in the organisation is designed and implemented in "one go", a pipe dream of early enthusiasts in their euphoria of having learnt a new trick. It is used here in the sense of taking a comprehensive view of interlockings systems/sub-systems and appreciating mutual input/output needs and building them as part of the design. It is only then that information is truly blended in the fabric of the total system.

(4) Common data flow: A great weakness in manual systems is the duplication and redundancy that exists of reporting into and out of functional areas and the corporate level. On the other hand, such a view should not delay the development of the MIS in a modular manner waiting for the pattern of data flow

in the total system. Hence, whereas the development of common data flow is an economically sound and logical concept, it may be prudent to live with a little duplication in order to make the system acceptable and workable. Effectiveness is of greater importance than efficiency; a pragmatic approach taking precedence over technical excellence.

(5) Planning element: MIS do not get positioned overnight but take years if not decades to implement. Some writers think of the philosophy of MIS as comparable to a compass where, even if the destination is never reached, the body corporate is being directed towards it. Some points relevant to its planning are:

— it must keep in step with the corporate plans and it certainly cannot exist in isolation;

— MIS must plan for future expansion and needs;

— designers must avoid obsolescence even before implementation; only sound and realistic planning can offset this aspect;

— a phased approach will get management approval e.g. even though a good integrated data base is desirable, and interval, without MIS as a consequence, would be totally unacceptable during the transition.

(6) Sub-system Concept: Even though a system is a single entity, it is, in complex organisation, made up of sub-systems. It is good practice to have a macro view to establish input/output relationships between sub-systems and build up the MIs in stages; what Bluementhal calls a Systems Perspective Approach.

This building block concept can even start at sub-system level.

(7) Flexibility and ease of use: No system can be static; also no one can really predict the future course of an organisation even two years hence; it should be naive to make pretence to have such omniscience. MISs must be built with the flexibly and resilience to absorb much, including the building in of possible courses. In this the building of a solid database would be a wise decision. If DBMS is used, tools are available today that will absorb much of future shocks; programming chores reduce with 4GLs (4th Generation Languages) and transitions would be almost instantaneous. Concurrent is the ability to have the end use as a partner in MIS, with good Menus and Help facilities.

(8) Data bases: The data base is the mortar to the sub-systems. The advantage of a singly point update are many and would justify the corresponding overhead on memory and time: accuracy, timeliness, consistency and security deserve mention.

(9) Distributed data processing: Large corporations, Government, the Services and similar other entities have a spatial distribution within a city as well as over the sub-continent. Even if there is a degree of autonomy, it is common to set up networks for more effective utilisation of resources (depots, warehouses and the like) and for planning monitoring and control. Included here would be the planning and positioning of a LAN (local area network) with "gateways" to WANs.

Place in the organisation

Data, being all pervasive, is considered a corporate resource. Its management and control, logically, must be vested at the highest possible level.

From the figure it would be clear that the control of Information must be at the highest level Typically :

— it may report to the VP (Management Services) a sin many companies;

— it may be a VP (Information Technology) as seems to be favoured in some Defence Service.

Where there are many ISs (Information Systems) and functional areas are discernible, it may be good practice to have "Committees of Direction" that perform the same function as the steering committee.

Even if there is move to have decentralised Information System it would be a wise policy to have control of data, exercising security and the laying down of Direction" that perform the same function as the steering committee.

Even if there is move to have decentralised Information System, it would be a wise policy to have control of data, exercising security and the laying down of standards being vested in a person at the highest level.

To illustrate TPS, MIS, and DSS, we will consider the case of a small business, Sara Morris Enterprises. We will use a small business so that you can readily grasp the nature of each different type of system. Realistically, however, Sara Morris is too small an organization to need OAS and ESS.

Sara Morris offers public seminars and provides consulting services for improving human communication.

Before starting her business, Sara worked as a clinical psychologist for a number of years. From time to time, she was asked to give motivational and other types of speeches. She is a gifted speaker, and Sara soon found that she was having more success making speeches than she was practicing psychology. She consequently decided to leave psychology and become a professional public speaker. Since she frequently received requests for follow-up consulting, she decided to offer consulting services as well.

Sara markets her seminars via direct mail, advertising, and professional associations. For direct mail, she maintains a list of customers from prior seminars, and she also buys mailing lists from time to time. She promotes herself through professional associations by speaking at workshops that they arrange. Sara's consulting business is an outgrowth of her seminars. Seminar attendees often request her services after meeting her and hearing her message. In fact, Sara has never needed to market her consulting services in any other way. Sara employs an administrative assistant. The assistant answers the telephone, responds to routine questions, maintains business records, arranges for the printing of seminar materials, makes reservations for seminar hotels, and makes travel arrangements. The assistant also helps with the preparation and mailing of marketing materials. The types of questions that Sara Morris and her assistant must answer to run the business. The first group of questions is concerned with operations This type of question is most often answered by a transaction processing system (TPS). The second group of questions is concerned with management of the company's affairs. These questions are usually answered by a type of MIS. Finally, the third group of questions is concerned with strategic issues. These questions are answered by a Decision Support System (DSS).

Observe that the questions are sorted in order of structure. The first group of questions can be answered by looking up data in a file. The middle-level questions involve processing of data. A question like "Should we increase prices?" is less quantitative than those in the second group. Analysis of data can help, but subjective judgment is also required. The last question is highly unstructured, and although its answer depends to some extent on information produced from data, it depends primarily on Sara's subjective feelings, beliefs, and attitudes.

It is easier to build information systems to answer questions for more structured questions. The last group of questions requires a balance of information from systems and subjective, human analysis. This situation is typical of all businesses. We will now consider the three types of information systems to respond to each of the categories of questions.

Transaction Processing Systems (TPS)

Transaction processing systems (TPS) support day-to-day operations. A few examples are ticket reservations systems, order-entry systems, check-processing systems, accounts payable systems, accounts receivable systems, and payroll systems. All of these systems help a company to conduct its operations and keep track of its activities.

TPS are the oldest type of information system. They were first developed in the 1950s in accounting departments of major corporations. They have been the workhorse of the information systems industry for the last 30 years.

The transaction processing (TPS) program generates two types of output. It sends messages back to the operator terminal, and it generates printed documents. For a ticket reservation system, for example, the program displays a message on the terminal that indicates which seats have been sold to a particular person; it also prints the tickets and, perhaps, a mailing label for sending them.

On-line transaction processing. There are two fundamental types of TPS. On-line systems involve a direct connection between the operator and the TPS program. On-line systems provide immediate results. They are used to process a single transaction at a time. An order arrives, say, by telephone call; it is processed at that moment; and the results are produced.

We will discuss computer hardware in the context of personal, work-group, and organizational information systems. For now, realize that the direct access storage unit in represents a hardware storage device that allows data to be accessed directly, in any order. This device allows, for example, the TPS program to read data about ticket reservations in the order that customers request them and not in the order in which they are stored on the file.

Batch transaction processing. Batch systems are a second type of TPS. Here, transactions are grouped together and processed as a unit. For example, in a check processing system, all of the checks received in a particular time frame, say, on a particular day, are grouped together. They are then sorted by account number and processed in a batch.

The architecture of a typical batch processing

application. As stated, the transactions are grouped into a transaction file and sorted. The batch is then read in order by the TPS program. This program reads the stored data, often called the old master file data, processes the transactions, and creates the new master file data. In the process, it generates reports. To match transaction records with master file records, the master file data is sorted in the same way tat the transactions are sorted.

For example, in a check processing system, the checks are batched and sorted by account number. The old master file, which is also sorted by account number, contains customer checking account data from the prior period. This data is updated to create the new customer master file. Reports produced include overdrawn accounts, monthly summaries, suspicious activity, and so forth.

Sara Morris Enterprises uses a TPS to keep track of customers, seminars, and course registrations. This TPS uses a set of programs called the Customer/Enrollment system, which Sara purchased from an independent computer consulting company.

Two of the screen displays that are presented by the Customer/Enrollment programs. These two screens show menus, which are lists of action choices. The assistant uses these menus to direct the system's activity. For example, to enroll a customer in a seminar, the assistant selects the first choice by placing the cursor a blinking bar) on the first item and pressing the Enter key.

Other choice are made in a similar way. For example, if the assistant wants to add, change, or delete seminar way. For example, if the assistant wants to add, change, or delete seminar data, the third item is selected. When this choice is made, another menu, called a sub menu, is displayed. At this submenu, the assistant is given the additional choices of adding, changing, or deleting seminar data.

Another type of screen display used for processing data by this system is a form. Such forms are the electronic equivalent of paper forms. An example form used for enrolling a customer in a seminar. The form is displayed when the assistant makes the first choice from the main menu. The assistant follows the procedure summarized to fill in this form. As shown, the assistant first determines whether or not the customer data exists. If not, the data is entered. Next, the assistant enrolls the customer in the seminar.

The Customer/Enrollment programs add, delete, change, or display values in these tables of data, depending on the choices selected from the Customer/ Enrollment menus. Additionally, the users have the option of querying these tables in an ad hoc fashion using a query processor. This is a program that allows users to pose questions for the data using a flexible language that is not difficult to learn.

The Customer/Enrollment system produces the three reports. These reports are most often displayed on the computer's screen, but either Sara or her assistant can print them if desired. Sara takes a copy of the Seminar report with her to the seminars to verify attendance. She also uses it to collect money at the seminar, as appropriate.

Sara's assistant uses the Customer report when responding to questions from customers and when collecting fees; she also uses it for other customer service functions. Finally, both sara and her assistant use the Course report when they need an overview of the year's activities.

This TPS helps Sara and her assistant to manage the operations of their business. It can be used to answer the first group of questions. It does not, however, address the remaining groups of questions. Other types of information systems are required for that.

Unfortunately, the term *management information systems* has two very different definitions. The first was defined as the development and use of effective information systems in organizations. This is the broad and encompassing definition. The second definition, and the one that now concerns us, is much narrower. The second definition identifies a type of MIS within the broad category of MIS.

The narrow definition of an MIS is an information system that facilitates management by producing structured, summarized reports on a regular and recurring basis. The output of such MIS are produced routinely and used primarily for controlling activities, although they can also be used for planning and organizing.

Such MIS are conceptually a level above transaction processing applications. They are not concerned with day-to-day operations, but rather are concerned with the management of activities that do support operations. Consider the example of ticket reservations. A TPS is used to take orders and print tickets. An MIS is used to measure and report the performance of each of the agent who sell tickets. Such an MIS keeps track of the number and amount of each agent's sales, and it regularly produces reports about agent effectiveness.

Usually, MIS applications process data that is generated by TPS and other internal information sources. The user submits requests for reports to the MIS programs. They, in turn, process the TPS data by aggregating and reformatting it, then producing reports. These reports are either printed or displayed on the manager's workstation.

In some cases, the reports are automatically generated. For example, the MIS programs may be written to produce a certain series of reports every Monday morning, at the close of every business day, or at the end of some other period. Sometimes the MIS application programs are written to look for exceptional conditions in the data and to produce reports if and when those conditions occur. Sara Morris, for example, might have an MIS application that prints the name and location of any seminar that does not have at least ten participants two weeks prior to the start of the seminar. Such reports are called exception reports.

In some cases, the MIS application does not read the operational TPS data directly. Instead, an extract of the TPS data is made, and the MIS application processes the extract. This is done for a variety of reasons-to provide security for the TPS data, to transfer data across computers when the TPS and the MIS operate on different machines, or to consolidate data to make MIS processing more efficient.

The MIS may also store and maintain data of its own. Some MIS applications have simple models of business activity that they use for processing data to generate information for the manager. If such models exist, they are static, so that the manager gets the same report every period.

Consider the second group of questions. To answer these questions, Sara Morris must take data from the operational, TPS applications, and use it to compute revenue, costs, and profit. She knows that her profitability depends on the seminar price, on the costs of food, rooms, and services in the hotel in which the seminar is held, and on the number of attendees. Sara has developed the following set of equations to determine profitability:

Profit = Revenue — Total-Expense

Revenue = Number-of-Attendees * Seminar-Price

Total-Expense = Fixed-Cost + Travel-Expense

Fixed-Cost = Hotel-Cost + Travel-Expense

Hotel-Cost = Daily-Meeting-Room-Cost * Number-of-Days

Travel-Expense = Airfare + (Daily-Lodging-Cost + $65) * Number-of-Days

Variable-Cost = Material-Cost + Food-Cost

Material-Cost = $40 * Number-of-Attendeess + $135

Food-Cost = (2 * Break-Cost + Lunch-Cost) * Number-Attendees * Number of Days

In these equations, the underlined variables are called independent variables. This means that the values of these variables do not depend on other variables, but rather on the actual number of attendees, travel expenses, and hotel prices. Given values for each of these variables, the profitability of a seminar can be approximated from the equations.

These equations are a simple model of the profitability of the seminars. These equations would be stored on the disk labeled MIS Data. This model is used to transform the raw data into information that will be helpful to Sara and her assistant. As stated previously, in an MIS, such models are static. They must be static so that the reports produced over varying time periods will be comparable.

These equations can be used before or after a seminar has been held. If they are used before a seminar, Sara inputs estimates of the independent variables and thus makes a projection of the seminar's expected profitability. She would make this projection to answer a question like, "Are there sufficient attendees to justify holding the seminar in Milwaukee next week?" Historical operational data may be used to calculate the estimates of the independent variables.

When the equations are used after the seminar, Sara inputs actual values from the operational TPS data. He equations then produce the actual profit or loss achieved. This process is followed to answer a question like, "What was he profit from the seminar in Boston?"

Although Sara could compute these equations by hand or write her own computer program to make the computations she did neither, Instead, she purchased a spreadsheet program that performs these calculations for her.

After a seminar is held, Sara inputs actual values of the independent variables and computes the actual profitability of the seminar. In this case, actual material and travel costs can be used and computed instead of the approximations in the equations. These actual values can be saved in the spreadsheet program. The profit and loss statements for all of the seminars she taught in the second (calendar) quarter of 1989, displaying both actual and estimated material and travel costs. This report not only helps Sara decide on the profitability of her seminars, but also helps her assess the accuracy of her projections and her model.

Historical data such as that will help Sara answer questions concerning her most profitable seminar topic. She can save actual values of costs and revenue using the spreadsheet, and then use the spreadsheet to determine the answers to her questions.

Decision support systems (DSS) are interactive, computer-based facilities for assisting human decision making. DSS differ from TPS and MIS in that they do not always support an ongoing process. Often, DSS are created to solve particular problems on an ad hoc processing basis. Unlike MIS, which are regular and recurring, the need for DSS can be irregular. In all cases, DSS are designed to facilitate the solutions of problems less structured than those of MIS and TPS. Therefore, the DSS must be less structured; flexibility and adaptability are essential.

Consider the need for DSS in a setting where ticket reservations are made. As stated earlier, TPS are used to support operations; MIS are used to facilitate the management of operations. A DSS would be used to study unstructured, possibly one-of-a-kind problems or opportunities. For example, suppose a strike by the musicians' union forces the cancellation of opera performances. The management of the opera association wants to know the impact on revenue of the cancellation of each performance. A DSS could be used to process the ticket agencies' data to produce this information.

In some ways, the term decision support facility would be more accurate than the term decision support system. DSS are not structured, finished systems as TPS and MIS are. Rather, DSS are collections of data and data-processing tools used to creatively manipulate data to answer unknown and often unexpected questions. Often times, too, the users of DSS do not have the assistance of professional information systems personnel. Instead, they employ the tools on their own.

Like MIS, DSS involve models of business activity. Unlike MIS, however, DSS models are often quite complex. They are also dynamic. They DSS user frequently changes the models to adapt them to the changing understanding and needs of a problem. The ticket agency, or example, may have a series of equations that predicts sales of tickets on the basis of type of performance, day of week, time of year, and so forth. As the strike progresses, the DSS users may add to or otherwise modify these equations to produce information that is important for negotiating a resolution to the strike. These models are stored as part of the DSS data.

Architecture of a DSS

Data from the organization's TPS and MIS applications is input to the DSS programs, along with data from external sources and DSS model data. As stated, the DSS may store and later reprocess its own model data as well. The user interacts with the DSS on-line; requests are made, models are created or adjusted, data is manipulated, and so forth. The outputs of the DSS program can be text, structured reports, or graphics.

A variety of programs support the DSS, including spreadsheet programs, personal database management systems (DBMS), word-processing packages, graphics generators, statistical packages, and other, special-purpose programs.

Briefly, Sara wants to know what will happen to her revenue and profitability if she raises prices. She believes an inverse relationship exists between price and attendance; if she increase prices, attendance will decrease. Her problem is that she does not know how much attendance will decrease. It may decrease only slightly, in which case the increase in prices will more than make up for lost revenue. On the other hand, it may decrease so much that the increase in prices will not make up for the lost revenue. She would like to know where the break-even point is.

In the spreadsheet, Sara attempts to simulate what would have happened in the second quarter if she had changed her prices. She uses the equations from the spreadsheet, but inserts the hotel and travel cost data from her second quarter seminars. She computes a baseline case using actual attendance and her current price. Then, she adds $100 to the price of the seminar and assumes 20 and 50 percent attendance reductions. These spreadsheets. With a 20 percent reduction, she earns about $7,500 more with the price increase. With a 50 percent reduction, she earns about $5,000 less.

Examining these results, she guesses that she would break even assuming a 35 percent attendance reduction. She entered that level of attendance and obtained the results. Her break even point is just about 35 percent. With this information, Sara now needs to make subjective business decisions. Will a $100 price increase reduce attendance more than 35 percent? Is it worth the risk? If she obtains, say, a 20 percent reduction in attendance, she will earn about $7,500 more. She will, however, meet

20 percent fewer people, and her consulting business may suffer. Sara will need to weigh these factors and other, similar ones before making the price change.

So far, Sara's DSS has involved only a small amount of operational data and a simple spreadsheet model. It is a simple DSS. To answer the question about the amount of attendance reduction due to a $100 increase, Sara might add other models of demand. She might also access, via programs on her computer, eternal sources of industry data that would tell her what other companies charge for seminars.

The next type of information system we will discuss is office automation systems. OAS are information systems that create, store, modify, display, and communicate business correspondence, whether in written, verbal, or video form. The prevalence of microcomputers in the office, along with a veritable explosion in new communications, computer, and storage products, are causing fundamental changes in the ways that offices conduct their business. At first, computer systems were used just for stand-alone word processing. Over time, however, computers were connected to one another. This connection allowed people not only to share word processing files but also to send messages to one another. With these developments, electronic mail systems were created in which office personnel could generate and send messages to one another. Also, since office workers could access the same files, they began to create electronic bulletin boards. These are essentially electronic posts on which people can leave public messages. All of these capabilities became even more exciting as high-quality graphics printers became affordable. With these printers, many systems gained the ability to process illustrations and graphics as well as text. Additionally, facsimile machines were improved and reduced in cost, so that documents containing text, illustrations, and graphics could be inexpensively communicated over telephone lines.

In parallel with these developments, computer technology was used to improve office voice systems. Office telephones were connected to more sophisticated private branch exchange (PBX) systems. Such systems allow workers to have voice mailboxes in which they can leave voice messages for one another. Finally, video systems were also developed. Large organizations developed video-conferencing capabilities so that people could communicate face-to-face without traveling. At first, such capabilities were used to connect a few executives in two or three locations. Recently, however, such systems have been used to connect thousands of people to the same presentations. IBM Corporation, for example, has connected over 100,000 people in a video conference to announce new products.

Doug Englebart, one of the pioneers in OAS, has stated.that the real power of OAS will not be realized by improving the productivity of existing office work. Rather, he believes the greatest benefit will be to enable people to think, communicate, and work together in new ways. OAS has the potential to change the way people way people view, conceptualize, and solve problems.

Hypertext systems are an example. With such systems, text, illustrations, graphics, data, programs, (and, in the long run, even audio and video segments) are integrated into an electronic document. Users can read such a document sequentially or at random just as books can be read. At the same time, however, these users can either follow many different preestablished paths through the document or they can establish their own paths. For example, multiple "threads" can be created for reading a repair manual; each threads is used for a different purpose. One might be used to make a particular repair, while another might be used to learn a particular skill.

Hypertext versions of encyclopedias and dictionaries are also being created. In these versions, the "see also" phrase in a reference book is replaced by a link to the actual text source. Thus, if a reader wants to follow the see-also link, he or she just touches a key and the material is presented immediately. With the hypertext versions, paging through multiple volumes is no longer necessary.

Unfortunately, today there are two important limitations in the development and use of OAS. First, much of the required equipment has been developed by different vendors working independently and using different standards. Because of this, machines often cannot communicate with one another. For example, it is difficult to connect computers to copying machines.

Part of the problem is technology, and part of the problem is that vendors sometimes have a negative incentive to connect to each other's equipment. IBM Corporation and AT&T, for example, are competitors. Neither company wants to operate on the same standard lest their equipment be readily replaceable by the other company's equipment.

The final result of this situation is that today OAS are divided into islands of capability. In, for example, there are realistically an island of linked computers, an island of copying equipment, an island of telephones, and an island of video-conferencing capabilities. Over time, these islands will undoubtedly be integrated as customers demand standardization and connectivity.

The second limitation concerns storage. Non-text data such as graphs or illustrations require substantially more storage than does text data. Voice and video data require even more. Consequently, it is not possible with today's technology to store large volumes of typical office documents in electronic form. Optical disk storage may provide a solution. Certainly it appears that some solution will be forthcoming during your career.

Legacy Systems develops and sells computer software products. Each of their products is accompanied by at least one user document, and most products have three or four different documents. A common document set consists of an installation booklet, a tutorial manual, a product capabilities manual, and a reference command summary book.

To develop documentation, Legacy has a staff of over 30 full-time writers. This staff is augmented by free-lance writers when necessary. Typically, a group of from three to ten writers is given the task of creating the documents for each product. More writers are needed to produce the documentation for new and complicated products than are required for revisions to products or for products with fewer features.

Although Legacy management devotes considerable time to product planning, the rapid changes in technology and in the software market sometimes necessitate dramatic changes in that plan. On these occasions, Legacy's Documentation group is often forced to write documents faster than they would like.

Since the documents often refer to the same examples and also refer to each other, it best if they are written sequentially. Although documents are often written sequentially, this is not always possible. When product development time is short, for example, writers are added to the project and the documents are developed in parallel. Because of the cross-references in the text, this situation can result in chaos if it is not carefully managed.

To facilitate parallel documentation development, the Documentation group uses a hypertext system to store and present the work in process.

At the first stages of the project, sections of documents are assigned to particular writers. The writers develop conceptual outlines of their sections and store these outlines in the hypertext system. All members of the writing team then review and comment on each other's sections. Sample screens for the planning of a new set of documents are shown. Observe that the cross-references are documented and that users are able to make comments about each other's work.

If a writer wants one section of the document to refer to another section, he or she indicates this to the hypertext system. The system will, in turn, establish a connection so that a reviewer of the document can readily obtain access to the cross-referenced material.

For instance, consider the development of an example that will be used by, say five different sections of the documents. When a writer wants to refer to the example, he instructs the hypertext system to establish a pointer to the example. The example, however, is stored in only one place. As the example is changed and developed, the sections that point to it automatically have access to the latest copy.

As portions of the document are finished, they are added to the hypertext system. Gradually, the document comes together as sections are completed. All the while, every writer has access to the latest version of completed work. In this way, inconsistencies become apparent sooner and less work is wasted or duplicated. The quality of the finished product is also higher. The hypertext system is also very useful in documentation changes for newly developed versions of the product.

Executive support systems are information systems that support the information needs of very senior executives. ESS summarize and present data at the highest levels of aggregation. Usually, they involve presenting reports in standard formats, and they often involve graphics.

ESS are the newest of the five categories. To date, they have had the least acceptance of the five types. One reason for this is that most executives started their careers prior to the widespread use of computer-based information systems. They did not study information systems in college, and they are reluctant users. Many, in fact, still consider the use of a keyboard as secretarial work. Furthermore, most executives have a number of extremely capable assistants who can produce written reports to meet the executive's information needs.

This situation is changing, and, during your career, computer-experienced business professionals will rise to senior executive positions. These professionals will probably be more open to-and may even expect-support from computer-based systems.

As, an ESS accepts data from all of the other types of information systems. It also accepts input from those who support the executive, such as administrative assistants. As you can see, the primary goal of an ESS is to obtain data from a variety of sources, integrate and aggregate that data, and display the resulting information in an easy-to-use, comprehensible format.

2

Computer Based Information Systems

The favourite buzz-word today is "information-explosion" and the buzz phrase is "informatics" (informatique if you were French or even a continental) and it is the keystone to the managerial structure.

Today, thanks to communications of an extraordinary swiftness and accuracy, any activity— be it the church, the military or business or even government—requires speedy action to react to even small changes in situation; hence the term "Information Explosion" because the improved communications also mean the receipt of a plethora of information to be scanned, screened and used for decision-making.

Thus "inforMation" has come to be regarded as another "M" to be managed; like the other Ms it was visualised as transcending functional boundaries. Some even give it a superior position *vis-a-vis* money although both are all pervasive.

Till this realisation took place, as a management specialist put it, it was taken for granted, like the sun: it was there and shining or it was not.

If this importance is accepted, one can visualise its control being exercised at higher levels in the hierarchy.

Facets of information

The very first general misconception to be corrected is the view that data and information are synonymous. Data is an occurrence, an event which, in conjunction with the environment, gives information. A train may whistle: it is an event and will mean different things to different people:

— to the man lying on the tracks, about to commit suicide, it may mean success;

— to the saboteur, waiting for the explosion, it may mean failure, since his charge has failed;

— to the gate keeper it may mean the last chance to close the level crossing etc.

In any organisation, there is always a large force employed in the various facets of information; often this may be 60% and over. Hence there is much scope for improvement and efficiency as also savings if the information function is improved.

Data generally goes through certain stages before it becomes Information, some of which may merge with each other:

— it is collected;

— it is "cleaned";

— sorted;

— communicated singly or in batches;

— manipulated (in its sense);

— displayed or stored or communicated through paper or electrically.

Although that aspect is dealt with separately, it is to be noted that in inter and intra stage, data is highly vulnerable to mutilation, loss and so on either accidentatly or deliberately.

Characteristics of information

Subjective

Information in subjective, concerned as it is with the recipient's needs, environment and so on. There is an ancient witticism that best brings out this aspect, where the barman pours beer into a mug and stops to refill his barrel and two friends view the beer mug that awaits

— the pessimist says "that mug is half empty"; and

— the optimist says "that mug is half full".

Hierarchical

A Company markets "Cellular Phones"; they have a "buy" and "make" policy and a strong quality control. On a certain data, twelve are bought and twenty-four are made and three are rejected. Let us check out the effect of this at various levels in the organisation:

— the Production Manager sees 12+24-3 i.e. 33 Cell Phones as below target;

— the Financial Controller sees is as Rs. 10,000x33 i.e. Rs. 330,000 as finished goods;

— the Chief Executive may see it as, say 1% of the turn over but cumulatively within his forecast;

At lower levels there will be sub-information systems:

— the foreman will have information that 'Ram made 8 and Shyam 12 etc.

— the purchase manager would have his information system to show- * "A" company delivered 2, * "B" delivered nil etc.

— the quality control's information system would record-* Ram produced 8 of which 1 was rejected, of Shyam's 12, rejects were 1 etc.

Presentation

A jumble of figures may be very confusing. The same data presented to management as a pie chart, would make things clearer.

Steam made its impact to give us the Industrial Revolution. Yet, 100 years were to pass before the laws of thermodynamics were propounded.

The "Chip" is said to have created waves in the field of information, if not a hundred, it will be some years before we have laws in informatics.

This is not to say we do not have some canons to postulate:

— Infosys must give information and not data;

— Every change to status, on occurrence, must be reflected in Infosys;

— Infosys must support the classical levels of managerial hierarchy, requiring no further processing at the recipient's end;

— Must take care of programmable decisions;

— Should support the diverse ratios of internal and environmental information needs at the various levels in the organisation.

The 80.20 rule

The study carried out on the need to go out of one's section, division, brings out some interesting facts as pictorically represented in Fig. 4.3; the consequence of this is the introduction of the concept of local Area Networks (LAN) and Wide Area Networks (WAN). Analysis of Fig. 1 would bring out the following facts:

— 80% of data for any decision-making, relevant to that part of the organisation, bet it the corporate office or any functional division/sub-division/or the lowest level, would be found within itself and only 20% has to be sought from outside;

— if terminals are in use, 40% of the total information needs, in that part of the organisation, will be accessible by it.

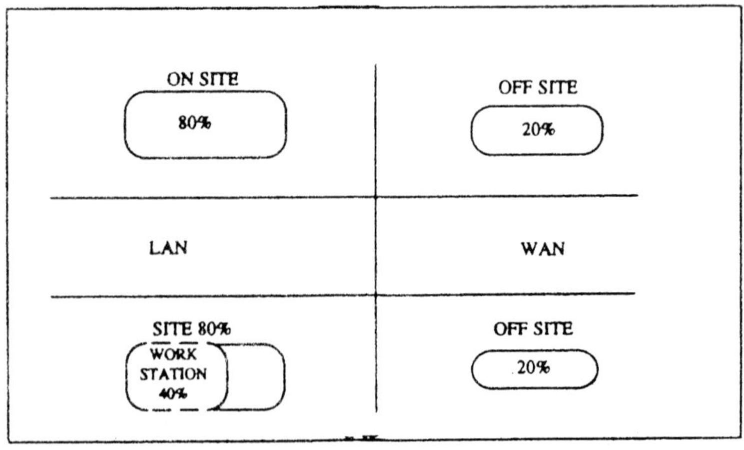

Fig. 1 The 80:20 Rule

Another source gives a detailed breakdown of three levels in an organisation. It will be seen that more than 50% of the time of an employee is spent in communication-voice, text and data. It is mentioned here because information is not just messages but all forms of intelligence transfer; in fact the world is heading towards transmission in digital format so that the same channel can be used for information transfer in all its wide range of existence.

Harnessing IT

The intention here is to focus the attention on the ways information technology can be brought into the organisation.

Approach

There are three ways of getting to INFOSYS (Information Systems): centralised; decentralised and distributed.

Centralised: In cases where one large computer is installed to meet the whole organisation's need, the advantages and disadvantages are as follows:

Advantages:

- good control of systems and resources;
- one policy and hence better standard;
- economy of scale achievable;
- corporate information likely to be of high standard;
- better scope of add-ons with improved technology;

- better untilisation of resources—people, space, equipment, money;
- may attract quality staff.

Disadvantages:

- end user feels cut off (it is somebody else's system);
- inevitable clash of priorities since it would be batch mode of operation;
- "all eggs in one basket" syndrome;
- little motivation to or cooperation from actual user; as a direct consequence, MIS will be of poor quality;
- the Manager-in-charge gets "power" in his hands and may lead to lopsided growth.

Decentralised: In cases where every user has a computer—a phenomenon possible with the PC explosion

Advantages:

- a degree of local autonomy and hence
- end user motivation high;
- end user participation multifold;
- controls optimal;
- priorities easily resolved, there being no contention;
- better response;

- extra capacity in small installations;
- meets the 80% rule well.

Disadvantages:

- likely duplication of effort and considerable "reinventing the wheel";
- redundancy of all types;
- information flows poor as in a manual system;
- incompatibility will exist amongst systems;
- information loses the "corporate" view;
- staff dilution likely;
- likely to be more expensive.
- Quotable quote of cynic "it has not only dispersed computing but also dispersed systems and people:increases cost and breeds incompetence".

Distributed: Distributed Data Processing (DDP); also called networking approach. This approach was the culmination of the various following developments:

— the systems approach;

— arrival on the scene of the cheap, ubiquitous, microprocessor;

— the arrival of LANs;

— digital communications.

It visualises nodes of computers linked to each other and also to further sub-nodes. Generally, they use protocols as laid down by international standards. .

Advantages of the two approaches seen earlier make this the most attractive approach; disadvantages are relatively few.

Processing methods

Refers to the way data is handled to provide information to management and can be seen as a trichotomy: batch, interactive and on-line. It would appear to keep in step with "approach" to information systems just covered above.

(a) *Batch:* Refers to the method by which the collection of all transactions occurring over a period is made and updating of the master files is done at set periods. The data processing staff acts of as "high priests" to "God computer".

The advantages and disadvantages would follow the pattern of the certralised approach. The following drawback, however, deserve special mention:

- numerous programmes have to be invoked, storage media have to be mounted/dismounted and, in fact, a high degree of manual intervention is implicity; all this is fraught with danger to security of data/ information;
- error correction is tedious and enforces time lags;
- all too often users get more details than they want;
- priorities get awry;
- managers tend to get disinterested and computer culture is one of the first casualties.

(b) *Interactive:* Here end users get access to the central computer and all "off-line" work is cut out. A high degree of data discipline is required and the existence of computer culture through the organisation is presupposed.

Security through good validation programmes is to be expected in this environment.

(c) *On-line:* Visualises a network of computers, with end users having access to it. It is not only the updation of data but on-line enquiries and facility to extend DSS that is implicit. A superset of on-line is real-time systems. Of course how real is "real" is a legitimate query. Fractions of a second could be the user conception of real time for Air Defence Systems; a second or so for Command and Control Systems; 5 seconds for passenger reservation.

Trackling information systems

The corporate strategy could be seen as trichotomy: total systems; integrate later policy; and systems perspective or building block policy. These are examined in the sections that follow.

Total systems: The organisation decides that every conceivable aspect of the information needs are designed and implemented in one final sweep.

Some facts that make this approach unattractive, tending to be disastrous, are:

— to implement in any reasonable time-frame, the resources necessary would be very high; often beyond the capacity of most organisations;

— during the interval, often three years or more, in large corporations, there will be no benefits of computerisation; this may be a deterrent to the development of computer culture; thus even before sub-systems are designed, they would be obsolete;

— thus even when installed, the MIS may not work to anybody's satisfaction.

Integrate later: The philosophy here is that wherever there is interest or scope, some computerisation is done without any thought to any other part of the organisation. The thinking is that some one, some time, will integrate-foolish dream as some organisations have found to their cost; often such integration is at a multi crore expense. Such "islands of computerisation" are a guarantee to the failure of a "systems" approach.

Systems perspective: Basically concerns large organisations with numerous functional areas. It visualises an analysis and synthesis profile that is the hallmark of a systems approach.

A two stage approach is visualised:

- a macro analytical study to establish functional areas, sub-systems etc., their input/output relationships, and mutual need for data.
- drawing up priorities, and building up on a building block concept.

The great advantage that would be apparent is the high degree of management participation that can be expected.

Classification of computer based information systems

Computer Based Information System can be classified according to their usage at the level of management hierarchy. This can be best explained by the help of

Antony's model of Management Pyramid and appropriate CBIS at each level. This is shown in Figure 2.

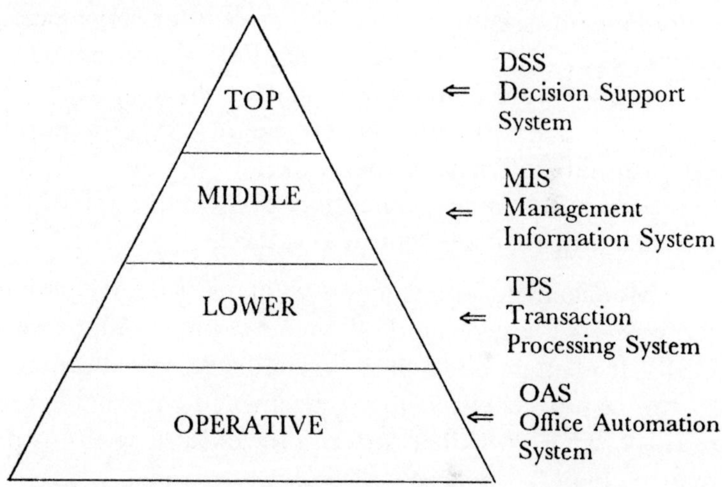

Figure 2: Levels of Management and Types of CBIS

The Computer Based Information Systems and generally classified into following types:

a) OAS : Office Automation Systems

b) TPS :Transaction Processing Systems

c) MIS :Management Information Systems

d) DSS : Decision Systems

The office automation systems originally were meant for clerical/secretarial level personnel in the organization and included things like word processing, photo copying and automating other office related activities. However, today with new generation of managers with high computer literacy they are encompassing working life of each and every one in the organization.

More details of OSA, TPS, and DSS are provided in forthcoming sections.

Transaction Processing Systems (TPS) are meant the automate transaction related activities in an organization which were earlier also known as EDP (Electronic Data Processing) and generally consist of things like sales invoices, payroll, billing etc. These are normally operational activities under purview of lower level of management, hence transaction processing systems are interact with management at this level.

Management Information Systems (MIS) is perhaps the most well known and all encompassing component of CBIS. It is intended to provide companywide information to the upper echelons of management hence it interacts mainly with middle and to an extent with upper management.

Decision Support Systems (DSS) are the CBIS which helps management in taking semi-structured/un structured decisions. Since these are normally taken at the highest level, such systems interact with top management.

Today, some of the advanced CBIS have features with incorporate both MIS and DSS and are termed as EIS (Executive Information Systems) since they by and large cater to information needs of middle-top executives of the organization.

There is another class of CBIS which is emerging are those which support group activities or team effort. These include systems such as audio conferencing, E-mail, video-conferencing and computer conferencing. Such CBIS are termed as Group Support Systems (GSS).

3

OFFICE AUTOMATION SYSTEMS

Tradition in the office environment is well-known to be a great force thereby, letter were typed, corrected, signed, mailed after the due process of registration; documents were elaborately linked and filed; executives travelled; decisions are made but the "seat of the pants"; intuition and hunch in fact continue even in the most modern organisations. On the horizon is the promise of better things to come through electronics and the ubiquitous "Chip". With the promise of a famine in paper, there seems a need to take a look at the "Office of the future", "the electronic office" or "office automation" and the many other titles that have been given to automating office functions. There is speculation that, in the 1990s the Electronic Office will be a 10 billion dollar market; by a conservative estimate. There are many definitions of this coming technology but that which follows would fit the bill—"it is a multifunction, integrated CBIS that lets many office activities to be performed in an electronic mode". The components are tabulated below :

Table 1

Entity	*Major functions*
1. Word processing	Facilitates the preparation of typed documents.

2. Electronic Main	Allows typed messages to be sent electronically.
3. Voice Mail	Allows spoken messages to be sent electronically.
4. Facsimile	Allows documents to be sent electronically.
5. Teleconferencing	Electronically bringing participants together without travel.
6. Telecommuting	Allows employees to work from homes.
7. Personal	Through workstations at the Manager's computing desk.
8. Computer terminal	Provides access to other components of the automated office.
9. Micrographics	Stores documents on microfilm for ease of storage and retrieval.
10. EPABX	The telephone exchange of the future, operating in digital mode that will support voice, text etc.

In this section we deal with srls 1 & 2 Only. Srls 3, 5 & 6 are futuristic as far as developing countries are concerned. Srl 4, Facsimile is improving day by day and is available as a service. Srl 9, is still to establish itself but COM is also on the horizon. Some EPABX (Srl 10) are already installed but a total Integrated Communications system is still in the future.

Some facts regarding office automation

Taking the average employees day (be he or she a manager, a clerk or whatever) in an office, everyone depends 50%, and more, time in communication of some form or other-voice, message, text and image. Another way of looking at it is, that there is a large work force involved in communications and processing of data; even a small improvement in its efficiency and efficacy will give an organisation substantial benefits; this has been the Standard under which Data Processing has been marching. Still another is the trend towards integration of Voice, Data, text picture and Message traffic; the era of digital Communications' ISDN & IDN.

If we could call that tenet No.1, tenet No.2. as a corollary, could be "users already on LAN/WAN should NOT be disturbed". This also arises from a study conducted on a few hundred organisations, the finding of which was, that 80% of the functions involving Data and its processing was of interest only within itself, only 20% were linked externally; and thereby was born the concept of Local Area Networks (LAN) and Wide Area Networks (WAN).

With the hold that Computers have taken in the developed countries, extending a terminal to a user is the rule rather than the exception. This leads to what we could term Tenet No.3 : Work stations with the user must have Universal access, thereby covering any plan to bring the office worker into this network/s.

If we look at Office automation is its wonder connotation, we should consider Facsimile (FAX), Teletext, Videotext, teleconferencing and telecommuting; not just the correspondence, record keeping and other clerical chores. We shall confine ourselves, in this chapter to the latter services which, with development of Digital communications and extensive Electronic exchanges, will be truly and Integrated Service to the user of data, the computer playing central role. The others are touched upon later.

Teletext is a superset of Telex in that speeds of 2, 400 bits/sec and more can be transmitted. It is based on computers and so messages will be stored and sent to the optimal satisfaction of the user: store and send when lines are busy; store and send at times of low rate; re-route etc.

Teletext uses the TV channel for giving updates on all kinds of services like air, train etc.

Videotext is a facility by which authorised users can have access to various databases through telephone lines.

Facsimile is the transmission of a document (like a map) by scanning and sending it as digital (although analogue ones exist) signals to be faithfully reproduced.

Teleconferencing is where the participants may be continents apart but can be brought together through telecommunications.

Network Office Architecture (NOA)

So we have decided to get the 'office' into electronic media; to use the Computer-person's jargon, we want an 'architecture' - The NOA.

Four key ingredients can be identified in the NOA:

— infrastructure;

— Basic facilities;

— Accessibility to the plethora of Applications Software;

— Ability to access the external world.

Infrastructure

The aim is to provide the proper interface between the Corporate, Divisional, local and so on resources and the Individual workstation. NOT just that but, have a set of rules, or standards, to ensure mutual exchange of Information.

The Interface has been the International Consultative Committee for Telephone and Telegraph. (CCITT)'s X-400 "Electronic Mail" récommendation that has been recognised by many manufacturers.

The idea is NOT to just pass messages but expect some action by the recipient; a Standard has emanated from the European Computer Manufacturer Association (ECMA) and is called the "Office Documentation Architecture" (ODA). The International Standards Organisation (ISO) is said to be using it as a Model for its Standard. Figures 4.7 gives a view of this nexus (in the benevolent sense) of X. 400 and ODA.

Basic facilities

To be acceptable, the ODA must provide certain basic facilities commonly met with in an office environment.

Typically, one can think among other things, of:

— Document creation;

— Filling;

— Messaging.

— Access to Software.

In this fourth odd years, Computers have brought in a staggering number of Operating Systems, Application Packages and so on.

NOA must provide the terminal user the ability to interact with as many such as possible.

Ability to access the external world

Universality demands this necessity since the user should have have the power to access, at his/her will, local computing power, the Divisional computing facility and every other hierarchical facility upto the Corporate computer, apart from the ability to use the same terminal for Office work.

The trend is to provide such a terminal along with facilities for voice, facsimile, text transmission etc.

The 'Engine' for NOA

The term has been used as a surrogate for the 'prime mover' or the agent that makes this possible. It will be an integrated package that will include among other things, the following facilities :

- Word processing;
- Electronic mail;
- Diaries and calendars;
- Reminder module;
- Directories;
- Distribution lists;
- Telephone logs;
- Folders;
- Application packages;
- Spread sheet;
- Image processing;
- Voice/Data/Image/Text Convergence;
- Graphics;

— Cad/CAM etc.

Practically every manufacturer is attempting to introduce these in an integrated manner. But the path to TOTAL integration from ONE terminal is still a long way off. Further, compatibility between manufacturers is an aspect that should pose concern to the average user.

Phased approach to implement Office automation systems

Practically every manufacturer has adopted a phased approach to the introduction of Office automation systems. Some of the phases are as follows:

Facilities offered in an integrated suite in the NOA Engine-Outline

1. Only a brief introduction is made since many will be within the ken of most Information Scientists.
2. WP. Word processing should meet two levels of competence—those with limited skills; those who are experts. Normal facilities met with are :
   - — word wrap;
   - — search and replace;
   - — centering;
   - — subscript/superscript;
   - — auto spelling check;
   - — manual/semi-auto/automatic pagination;
   - — headers & footers; choice for odd/even/first page;
   - — forms creation/fill;
   - — automatic footnotes;
   - — insert/overtype mode choice;

— operation in blocks of text Eg delete/move/copy/underline/case/bold superscript etc.;

— search for 'sound alike' when uncertain of spelling;

— automatic section numbering & table of contents;

— parameters like page length/headers/footers/formats of page numbering/section numbering etc. of documents;

— storage of multiple texts for subsequent recall and insertion;

— simple arithmetic;

— revision tracking and amendment highlighting;

— move/copy/delete etc. by column;

— justifying/partially justifying/margins;

— immediate formattings so that users can see, interactively, exactly what will be printed, displayed;

— do/undo equivalent to 'stet' etc. etc.

3. Electronic Mail. Apart from sending messages, electronically, to other users within the organisation :

— automatic logging of copies;

— retaining them for specific periods;

— authenticating them with a 'signature';

— noting time of despatch;

— send to individuals/groups;

— provide unlimited "mail boxes";

— set up precedences and priorities;

— provide levels of Security and privacy etc.

4. Diaries/Calendars. The executive has to keep tag on his appointments and engagements.

— Some facilities visualised

Phase 1:

— give simple Word processing capabilities;

— Introduce some OA software e.g

— for Storage, text retrieval etc.;

— Electronic Mail;

— to access value added external Services;

— And other such, packages

Phase 2:

— Select a well-known package;

— Provide X 400.

Phase 3 :

— Introduce image processing package.

— Integrate Voice/Data at a workstation.

Phase 4 :

— Introduce image processing package.

— Integrate Voice/Data at a workstation.

Phase 5:

— Integrate all communication modes at one work station; this is more or less futuristic.

The Electronic Office is here but not yet in any tangible fashion except in developed countries. We cannot afford to miss the boat and be decades behind. Managers and Specialists must realise the importance and plan for it.

One last word. Let Security NOT be forgotten in all that euphoria of keeping up with the advanced nations.

4

Transaction Processing Systems

Computer-based information systems use computers to store data about organisations and make this data available to the organisations personnel. Let us take as an example a very simple computer-based information system, where a person has a small computer who enters data into that computer. The data may be a simple record of daily sales. One entry is made for each sale and the entry states the item sold, the quantity of items sold and the sale price. Each entry is stored as a record on a life on the computer disk. At the end of the day, the computer can generate reports from the stored file showing total sales and sales trends. The user can use this information to make decisions. In this simple example of a computer-based information system, the person has processed the data of daily sales and generated an information about the transactions he had during the day. A transaction is, thus, a record of some well-defined single and usually small occurrence in an organisation. Thus a sale, a bank withdrawal or deposit or a single seat reservation results in a transaction, as does the placement of an order for parts.

Working of a TPS

Transactions are input into the computer to update computer files or databases. The transaction system first checks the transaction to ensure that no erroneous data are input into the computer. The transaction must then pass through a number of checks. The first check is usually called an edit, which ensures that all the needed data are included in the transaction in a correct format. This is followed by checks which ensure that the input data are consistent with existing data in the database. Once all the checks are made, the transaction is used to update the database.

The transaction system provides responses to the user as the transaction progresses through the system. Any errors and inconsistencies as well as the result of a final updated database are reported. Responses can be provided in a number of ways, depending on the transaction system mode.

Transactions may be input in on-line or in batch mode. In the on-line mode, transactions are input into the system as soon as they arise. In the batch mode transaction are collected into batches which may be help for a while and input into the computer later. A common example of on-line systems are bank transactions. A bank withdrawal is entered directly into the computer system at the time the withdrawal is made. The person who entered a transaction receives an immediate response from the computer. Thus the system will immediately inform the operator if there are sufficient funds to meet a withdrawal.

Batched transaction systems do not provide such immediate responses. In a batch system, a number of transactions are collected before entry into a computer system. For example, a number of hourly work slips may be collected during the day and gathered into a batch. This batch will be input into the computer system at the end of the day and the user will obtain any responses on the next day.

Typical TPS

If one looks at typical organisations, one will find that they have many common features. Consequently, their transaction processing systems will be very similar.

In a typical organisation with three levels of management, we find that these organisations have the following interactions:

— Top management establishes policies, plans and objectives

— Middle management converts these to specific revenue, cost and profit goals,

— Operational management has specific schedules and measurement yardsticks.

Transaction processing system applications

Applications: Airline booking system

Records of seat availability on all its planes will be kept by an airline on a central computer. The computer is linked *via* terminals to a worldwide system of agents. Each agent can gain access to the flight records and within seconds make a reservation in respect of a particular flight. This reservation is recorded immediately so that the next enquiry for that flight (following even microseconds after the previous reservation) finds that particular seat or seats reserved. The computer records reflect an accurate picture of the airlines seating load at all times because there is no time lag worth mentioning.

The computer would then output information for the production of the customer's ticket and flight instructions, on confirmation on the booking by the customer.

Each booking is a separate transaction which is processed immediately i.e. not batched. This is, therefore, an on-line transaction processing system (OLTP).

Features of OLTP

1. Response time : The service given by an on-line transaction processing system can be measured in terms of response time. This is the time taken by the system to respond to an input, e.g. the time interval between the foressing of the last key by the operator of a VDU and the display of the required (updated) information.

2. Traffic pattern : An important feature of an on-line transaction system is the traffic pattern, i.e. the volumes of data being input, the times at which they are input, the types of input and places at which they are input.

3. Reliability : As on-line transaction processing systems operate automatically, and extremely high standard of system reliability is required.

   (a) Program protection : Many programs occupy main storage simultaneously and the integrity of each program must be protected.

   (b). File Security : Duplicate files will probably need to be kept and in addition their contents will be dumped at intervals.

These measures will aid re-construction should the need arise.

(c) Stand-by-machinery: In the airline application two CPU's would be required one of which is operational and the other a stand-by machine would automatically come into use.

(d) Security : The entire system has to be protected against unauthorized access and also data security has to be maintained.

Hardware software considerations

In the operation of an airline booking system the following have to be considered while selecting the hardware and software:

(a) a large main storage requirement to accommodate systems software and application progress. Also required will be an area to use as buffers for queuing of messages.

(b) Direct access storage of large capacity as backing storage.

(c) A real time operating system to handle different operations simultaneously.

(d) A data communication system linking the many terminals with the CPU.

Cost

On-line transaction processing systems are usually designed for a particular application and are extremely costly. Cost will vary with the service one wishes the system to provide. The better the service (i.e. the shorter the response time generally) then the more costly it becomes in terms of hardware and software etc.

Application : Large corporate organisation

Depending upon the type of organisation any number of

the following functions of the organisation may be supported by the transaction processing system :

(a) Finance and accounting

(b) Manufacturing

(c) Marketing

(d) Personnel

In order to support the processing needs of such organisation the transaction processing system may be a desktop personal computer or a large system, but the system has to be versatile, reliable and efficiently organised.

Features of the system

Specific features may include:

(a) **Distributed facilities:** There may be a mainframe computer at the head office acting as host to smaller computers at divisional offices. A divisional office could deal with marketing or production say. A lower level of the distributed system might handle office automation by means of routine data entry linked to the main computer.

(b) Integrated files or data bases: The integrated file processing can be exploited so that the receipt of orders may automatically give rise to, the ordering of materials, the movement of stock, the scheduling of production, the control of production and the distribution of manufactured goods.

(c) Combinations of different processing methods: Run of the mill stock control and payroll applications may be placed by batch method of transaction processing, while enquiries, orders, booking etc. are being handled by on-line transaction processing.

Hardware, Software Considerations

The following have to be considered while selecting the hardware and software:

(a) The distribution of processing, communications and data.

(b) The use of many different types of software to support the varied processing needs.

5

Decision Support Systems

In this section we will look into an approach for designing a comprehensive and integrated DSS that encompasses decision aiding techniques based on mathematical/statistical models. Also in this chapter we will provide a library framework for identifying the tools and techniques appropriate for the three levels of management (operational, tactical and strategic).

Functional support systems

Decision Support Systems use a variety of tools for managerial decision-making. To support management's practical functions, research in management information systems, management support systems (MSS), and DSS has produced tools, techniques and methodologies. It is the integration of these various tools, techniques and methodologies which constitutes a Functional Management Information system, which provides in an organised manner past, present and speculative information for supporting the planning control and operational function of an organisation in the given time frame thereby aiding in decision-making. Thus, a functional information system must incorporate transaction processing, MSS and DSS for planning and control purposes, where a functional MSS is an integrated set of decision and operational support tools that aid managerial control and a functional DSS is an integrated set of decision support tools that aid managerial planning.

Techniques for development of a successful DSS:

Operation research and management sciences provide tools best used for problems containing specific attributes of the conditions or situations.

Statistics provide several tools that are used to investigate strength and type of relation between values of interest in the corporate environment. Statistical models can explain the past behaviour of selected values of interest and predict possible future implications for managerial decision.

A new class of tools-expert systems and natural language systems, based on AI techniques has begun helping managers. These tools rely on stored knowledge concerning specialized topics to give advise or interpret requests for information.

Design of a functional DSS

In practice, designing a DSS for either planning or control purposes is difficult as the information needs of functional areas within an organisation are varied. A top-down design for a DSS addresses this difficulty.

In this DSS design information represents planning specifications for each level of management throughout the organisation. Each level of management provides increasingly more detailed requirements for enacting the organisations functional plans. Thus, an integrated DSS must in corporate different combinations of tools for the different managerial levels.

DSS tools for the three management levels

Operational managers rely heavily on quantitative tools (inductive and positivistic) as decision-making aid, as the focus of managerial effort is on daily problem solving activities. With advances in AI, operational managers also use qualitative decision support in addition to the traditional quantitative tools.

Tactical managers establish policies which act as guidelines for operational managers and familiarize strategic managers with problems arising from strategic decision-making. Therefore, they use both quantitative and qualitative tools.

Strategic managers also use both tools, but predominantly qualitative tools (Heuristic and Deductive) as the information required is largely subjective at this level.

Decision support tools for operational management

For operational management, numerous decision support tools are available which are—

(a) Material requirement planning (MRP), a method for ordering and maintaining materials in inventory, and is a systematic approach to identify cost-beneficial ways of inventoring materials.

(b) Linear Programming helps in problems involving allocation of limited resources and evaluating alternatives to satisfy singular or multiple objectives.

(c) Queuing theory is used in planning many of the organisations daily activities to determine economically beneficial queues, such as queues that occur in the manufacturing of goods.

(d) Descriptive statistics are used to estimate a parameter

of interest and the dispersion of values associated with that parameter. These estimates are made for the critical environmental factors to plan the daily operations of the organisation.

(e) Correlation Analysis is used for calculating the relationship between values for parameters of interest, such as parameter values describing current conditions facing managers.

(f) Analysis of Variance describe the variance between two or more variables of interest.

Decision support tools for tactical management

Tactical management similarly use decision support tools like—

(a) Network Analysis, a pictorial tool for identifying and sequencing tasks help managers plan and control tasks necessary for successful operation of the organisation. With network analysis, tactical managers can identify these tasks critical for successful implementation of corporate activities.

(b) Transportation problem are used for planning the distribution of various facilities and resources.

(c) Maximum flow or distance is a tool for identifying the most economically beneficial flow through, or distances between, object is of interest. This facilitates in determining the most preferred flow of goods or services through an area or object for which the organisation must conduct business.

(d) Dynamic programming is a tool used to ensure that the organisation's operations follow the appropriate course of actions relative to the prevailing conditions and the decisions of strategic managers.

(e) Correlation analysis is used to see if there is a

relationship between a factor over which it has control and other factors beyond its control.

(f) Analysis of variance is used as supporting information in deriving policies. Such results can determine if performance levels deviate under different sets of circumstances.

(g) Regression analysis derives a "line of best fit" from a distribution of data values for which there is an interest such as previously unidentified trend. The equation of the trend line can estimate values for an item of interest on the basis of the known values for influential variables. Tactical managers frequently use this equation to estimate the value of unknown variables that may influence plans for implementing strategic manager's decisions.

(h) Discriminant analysis identifies variables that may discriminate between two or more objects of interest. With the results of discriminant analysis, tactical managers can influence unruly variables to behave in fashion more harmonious with strategic manager's decisions.

(i) Factor analysis can reduce the number of variables (within or outside of the organisation) to deal with during interaction with an item of interest.

(j) Cannonical Correlation generates linear combinations for separate items of interest and determines the correlation between these linear combinations. Tactical managers use cannonical correlation to compare trends discerned from implementing plans for carrying out the decision of strategic managers. This information obtained from cannonical correlation helps in adjusting these plans to ensure conformity with the direction of strategic manager's decision.

(k) Multidimensional scaling is a tool for transforming unidimensional expressions of relationships into multidimensional expressions of these same relationships. With this tools, tactical managers can determine the significant relationships they must deal within their planning efforts.

(l) Gaming theory is a mathematical theory based on the general features of an organisation's competitive situations, placing considerable emphasis on the decision-making process of its competitors. Tactical managers can use this approach to answer the "What if" questions concerning adversarial situations within the strategic plans of the organisations.

(m) Markov processes are tools employed to determine global probabilities associated with the occurrences of events related to changing propensities of objects of interest. These global probabilities can then be used to determine more appropriate courses of action for the organisation.

(n) Non-linear programming is a compilation of various tools, such as quadratic programming and convex programming, used to help managers derive a solution to problem modelled with non-linear functions.

Decision support tools for strategic management

Strategic managers use decision support tools in the same way as tactical managers, except for the fact that strategic managers use highly aggregated data and they use these tools to support decisions that can change the organisation's entire nature of operations.

At tools for decision support

The one set of decision support tools applicable for all

levels of management, and in all functional areas, are the products at AI techniques-expert systems and natural language systems. With the growing complexity of organisational problems human expertise is falling short. Expert system tools store and provide the factual and heuristic knowledge of one or more human experts and it is impervious to emotional and other pressures which adversely affect human judgment.

Natural language systems are used to access a DBMS or other DSS tools. They are a vital aid for present day managers who have neither time nor the inclination to master the intricacies of conventional data base retrieval languages.

There were in brief some inputs on major types of CBIS. Many new types of CBIS such as Expert Systems and Nueral networks are converging. In time to come all these CBIS will emerge to more dynamic and will have companywide applications.

6

Planning and Control of the MIS Function

In recent years, management information systems (MISs) have become an important corporate resources. Some companies have MIS budgets that amount to 1 to 4 percent of sales. In the banking industry, it is not uncommon for an MIS budget to represent up to 16 percent of operating expenses. It has been reported that during the last four years MIS related costs have grown at an annual rate of 16 percent. There is little doubt that the relative amount of financial resources dedicated to MISs has increased significantly during recent years and that this trend is likely to continue in the foreseeable future. Nolan estimates that the computer expenditures of large companies will have increased six- to eightfold during the current decade.

The computing power of equipment has increased 18 times in the last ten years. Computerized MISs have become so important to some industries that many organizations could not survive without their effective functioning. For most organizations, MISs are no longer confined to a well defined organizational unit, often referred to as a data processing or computing center MISs now transcend the organizational boundaries of the computing center and reach almost all parts of the organization. Personal computers (PCs) are used throughout organizations. Networks link PCs, and central data bases can be easily accessed as PCs are linked to mainframes. Office automation and telecommunication installations are constantly on the increase.

This growing importance of the MIS function is reflected by the increasing number of MIS executives who have joined the ranks of top executives. Chief information officers (CIOs) now have responsibilities that go far beyond those of traditional directors of MISs. They often report to a company's chief executive officer. They concentrate on long-term strategic planning for MIS resources and the contribution of these resources to a company's success. They are in charge of the company's information technology, which includes data processing, office systems, and telecommunications. The day to day operations of the various systems are often left to subordinates. One of the chief functions of today's CIO is to establish an effective liaison between MIS users and data processing (DP) professionals. Their mission includes looking for ways to use information technology to gain a competitive advantage, creating new products and services, reducing costs, and assisting in the formulation of new strategies.

A glance at the MIS literature shows an increasing preoccupation with the management of this important resource. The purpose of this chapter is to review the planning and control issues involved and to propose a systematic approach for the design of a management central system (MCS) for the MIS resource.

Planning and control systems

Anthony, Dearden, and Bedford's framework for

planning and control systems has been widely accepted in the management accounting and MIS literature. We will briefly review their framework and then try to apply it to the planning and control of a modern MIS.

Anthony, Dearden, and Bedford define management control as "all methods, procedures and devices, including management control systems, that management uses to assure compliance with organizational policies and strategies." They define a management control system (MCS) as "an organized systematic process and structure that management uses in management control."

The control system, therefore, helps to direct and guide the organization to its desired goals. The management control process for any action consists of three phases: planning, execution, and evaluation. Anthony, Dearden, and Bedford make a distinction between three basic categories of management processes:

1. Strategic planning is the process of deciding on the goals of the organization, and the formulation of broad strategies to be used in attaining these goals.

2. Management control is defined as the process by which management assures that the organization carries out its strategies.

3. Task control is the process of assuring that specific tasks are carried out effectively and efficiently.

It is important to note the difference between management control and task control. Task control applies to activities where approximate optimal input/output relationships exist. Once these are known, routine decision rules can be developed and enforced. Examples include inventory management systems using economic order quantities (EQQs), automated plants, accounts receivable processing, etc. No managerial judgement is needed once a precise or "optimal" way of doing things is established. Management control involves situations where judgement is needed to determine the "right" cost or level of services. Input/output relationships are not known or cannot be measured. Examples include employee benefits, the size of a legal department, the level of R&D activity, continuing education, the work of staff units, and many MIS activities.

Even a brief scrutiny of a modern MIS organization shows that its management is involved in all three basic management activities. From both a management control and MIS viewpoint, it is of interest to review the characteristics of information needs for these basic management processes. They are shown in table 1.

Table 1

Characteristics of information	*Operational control*	*Management control*	*Strategic planning*
Source	Largely internal	⟶	External
Scope	Well defined, narrow	⟶	Very wide
Level of aggregation	Detailed	⟶	Aggregate
Time horizon	Historical	⟶	Future
Currency	Highly current	⟶	Quite old
Required accuracy	High	⟶	Low
Frequency of use	Very frequent	⟶	Infrequent

It is important to note that the information needs for these three basic managerial activities are quite different. The information needed for managing well defined tasks is probably of little use for higher-level decision making. Ideally an MCS for the MIS function should try to assure, among other things, that each MIS subsystem provides relevant information for each level of managerial activity. Another very useful concept in the context of management decision making is Simon's (1960) idea of breaking down the decision process into three phases: intelligence (information gathering); inventing, developing, and analyzing possible courses of action; and the choice activity. Simon develops the notion of structured and unstructured problems. Fully structured problems are those where all three phases are structured. This means that algorithms and decision rules can be used. An unstructured one is where none of the three phases is structured.

Management control structure

The concept of a responsibility center is at the core of a management control system. The structure of a management control system is made up of different kinds of responsibility centers.

Table 2

	Operational controls	*Management controls*	*Strategic planning*
Structured	Accounts receivable	Budget analysis engineered costs	Tanker fleets mix
	Order entry	Short-term forecasting	Warehouse and factory location
	Inventory control		

Semi-structured	Production scheduling	Variance analysis overall budget	Mergers and acquisitions
	Cash management	Budget preparation	New products planning
Unstructured	PERT/COST systems	Sales and production	R&D planning

Every responsibility center has inputs and outputs. In the case of an MIS department the inputs consist of equipment dedicated to information processing and the work done by its employees. These inputs can be measured in quantitative accounting (costs) or non-accounting terms. Qualitative inputs measures are also used when appropriate.

Outputs are the various services rendered to users. They can also be measured by quantitative measures or by qualitative measures.

Types of responsibility centers for MIS departments

MIS departments can be organized as expenses centers, profit centers, or investment centers. All three types of responsibility centers are used for MIS departments. Expense centers measure inputs in terms of their costs. They may be engineered, discretionary, or allocated expense centers. When the required input of an expense center can be predetermined we speak of an engineered expense center. If managerial judgement is used to determine the right amount of cost then we are dealing with a discretionary expense center. When the cost of an expense center is allocated to users we have an allocated expense center. Such an allocation of cost is often referred to as a charge back. If services are "sold" to users at a price that exceeds cost, the department essentially becomes a profit center. If in addition to "selling its services" the MIS department assumes full responsibility for its investments, the department becomes an investment center. In the latter case one could view the MIS department almost like an independent business. Before discussing the pros and cons of these types of MIS responsibility center we will briefly review the typical functions and activities performed in an MIS department.

MIS depart-ment functions

The MIS departments of most organizations perform similar functions. These functions or activities usually include the following: systems development, operations, and technical support. In addition, there is an MIS administrative function with the usual responsibilities of supervision, security, accounting and finance, personnel and administrative support.

Systems development Over the years there has been an important evolution in the objectives of these systems. Early systems had an accounting orientation. These systems continue to exist. They became what may be called operational support systems. This included tasks such as inventory and production scheduling. The idea of decision support systems (DSSs) began to take hold in the 1980s. DSSs are computer-based interactive systems that help decision makers utilize data bases and models to solve problems. These systems thus aim to support primarily "higher" levels of decision making.

Recently there have been a number of proposals for strategic support systems (SSSs). Developing such systems would include the search for and the development of information technologies to help in shaping and supporting strategic plans, especially those that aim at giving the firm a competitive advantage. Thus, a research and development function is also included in systems development.

Today the MIS consists of many subsystems. These include financial accounting systems, management control support systems, planning support systems, and decision support systems. These systems coexist with varying degrees of interdependence. They often use common data bases, hardware, and software.

Operations These include mainly repetitive activities that are often compared to factory operations. They include the scheduling and control of computer operations. This will involve establishing priorities and generally assuring effective and efficient operation of the central processing units (CPUs); the maintenance of tape and disk libraries, operation of CPUs, and peripheral equipment; and the maintenance of both systems and application software.

Technical support This usually includes various kinds of technical assistance for the above MIS activities. It also includes MIS data administration; teleprocessing and telecommunications management; and the management of related facilities.

All MIS activities require close cooperation with users. Many of the systems and support related activities deal with introduction of new technologies and are of an experimental and research nature. If these principal MIS activities, regardless of where in the organization they are located, are under unified management control we have a clear line of demarcation between the MIS unit as a provider of services and the various users of the services provided. From a management control view, we would be dealing with a clearly defined responsibility center. This is usually no longer true in today's MIS configuration. MIS services and facilities are no longer under the exclusive control of the MIS department. This is especially true with the arrival of end user computing (EUC). Users have their own terminals and computers, their own software, and frequently their own data bases. User facilities may have access to the central processing unit. The MIS department's services include technical assistance and the training of end users. In recent years there has been a trend from the traditional data processing (DP) centers toward users in terms of both physical resources and function. Nolan refers to this as moving from a DP driven stage to a user driven advanced stage of MIS development. MIS departments, therefore, no longer have complete control over the operating costs and the investment of a company's global information system.

MIS Costs

MIS costs can be classified in different ways. Two basic categories would be personnel costs, and costs related to the operation of the computing and communications equipment. There has been a clear decline in the relative importance of equipment related costs. It is estimated that, on average, these now amount to less than 40 percent of total costs. Personnel costs, on the other hand, account for an ever increasing share of the total costs.

These costs could also be broken down by the different kinds of activities described earlier. This is usually done for budgeting purposes. The aggregate costs of running an MIS department are typically determined by top management. All costs are essentially fixed. They will not vary from budgeted amounts, except in the case of unforeseen emergencies. It is therefore difficult to allocate these costs in any realistic way to the services rendered to users.

While some of these fixed costs can be directly traced to specific services we have many costs that are common to many services and certain overhead costs that are common to all services. Even if we identify the traceable fixed costs of a service we must make some assumptions as to service volumes to arrive at some kind of a unit cost. All common and joint costs would have to be allocated to services on some rational basis. This is impossible to do in practice. These factors are responsible for the often reported problems with allocation or charge back schemes. Because the bulk of the costs are fixed (i.e. they will not be affected by either the quality or the quantity of services performed), they measure neither the effectiveness nor the efficiency of an MIS department. More subtle approaches are needed.

Transfer prices

Internal transfer prices must be established when an MIS depart-ment is organized as a profit or investment center. Management accounting generally distinguishes between cost-based, market-based, and negotiated transfer prices.

For cost-based transfer prices one would ideally develop a standard cost for each service that would exclude MIS depart-ment inefficiencies. In order to generate a profit for the MIS department, a reasonable profit margin must be added to the standard cost of the services. The reasonableness of this margin is difficult to establish and may therefore be contested by dissatisfied users. The biggest difficulty cost figures for the services rendered. Because of the prevalence of fixed and joint costs this will require many arbitrary assumptions with regard to activity levels and allocation bases. The resulting transfer prices will often be contested by users. Market-based transfer prices have the problem that established market prices for outside MIS services are usually not available. Even standardized services, for which outside market prices may exist, are seldom truly comparable because of special features, size, frequency of processing, etc. Often these services may be priced by the suppliers on a marginal costs basis and may therefore not be suitable.

The management accounting literature often proposes the use of dual transfer prices. For example, users would be charged for only the standard cost of services while the MIS department is credited with the standard cost plus a fixed markup, with the difference between the two prices being charged to some cor-porate overhead account. The users have the advantage of not being charged for a potentially debatable internal profit margin, while it is possible to evaluate MIS performance in terms of profits, return on investment, or residual income. The knotty costing problems mentioned earlier are still present with this approach.

In many companies transfer prices for goods and services exchanged between divisions or departments are not established by a centrally determined mechanism or formula, but are negotiated by the parties concerned. Such an arrangement works best when users are free to use outside services if they are not satisfied with what is available within the organization. Only then will the resulting transfer price truly be the result of an arm's length negotiation. Unfortunately arrangements that give both parties equal negotiating positions are rarely present for MIS services. For most MIS services there will be no suitable outside sources and, even if they were available, dependence on outside sources for critical MIS services may not be desirable.

Factors that make MISs different

In this section we will try to summarize the principal factors that make it difficult to apply traditional management control and responsibility concepts to the planning and control of MIS activities:

1. MIS services will continue to need to work with new technologies. Major efforts must be devoted to the assimilation of new ways of doing things. Therefore, many MIS activities are of an experimental or research nature.

2. MIS services include activities failing under all three of Anthony, Dearden, and Bedford's basic management activities. Some are important for strategic planning, most would fall under management control, and some fall under task control.

3. MIS services include many different subsystems that vary greatly in relative importance. Some may be of strategic importance, requiring top management participation in their design and operation; others may perform only simple support functions.

4. The global nature of MIS services transcends organizational boundaries. Responsibility for the cost of equipment and operation is at least to some extent shared with user departments.

5. MIS activities are very diversified. Some of the resulting costs could be classified as engineered, while the bulk would fall into the discretionary category.

This analysis shows that the traditional control structures of management accounting cannot be readily applied to the MIS function. The characteristics of MIS activities vary significantly. Some are routing, predictable, and repetitive. Others, although non-routine and non-repetitive, still have fairly predictable outcomes. Still others are unique and highly experimental, very much like basic or applied research. All of them take place in a constantly changing technological environment, in which today's satisfactory solutions may be totally inadequate tomorrow.

The MIS environment varies greatly from industry to industry. In some industries, certain MIS functions may be of strategic importance. In others, MISs fulfill only a support function. But even the relative importance of the MISs in an organization is not stable over time, but may change rapidly. A further complication is the non-comparability of MIS functions in the same industry. They evolved differently, are not standardized, have different levels of sophistication, and are greatly influenced by company specific factors. Appropriate planning and .ontrol approaches, if they are to be effective, must take all these differences into account. In the following section we shall try to systematically classify these factors. On the basis of these classifications we shall propose guidelines for the establishment of effective MIS planning and control structures and processes.

Stages in the assimilation of MIS technologies

The rapid changes in computer and telecommunications technologies have imposed upon the MIS specialist the need constantly to update his knowledge. MIS departments have had to cope with these changes, we new technologies had to be assimilated just to keep current. During the last years changes in computer technology have increasingly impacted not only on the MIS department, but on other parts of the organization as well.

More than ten years ago. Nolan and Gibson published their stage theory of computer systems organization and management. Subsequently Nolan refined and adapted this stage theory to fit the environment of the 1980s. Essentially, the theory demonstrates than an organization progresses through various stages while assimilating computer technology. This progress can be shown through an organizational change concept, developed by Schein, that seems appropriate for our discussion. Schein distinguishes four phases of technology assimilation.

1. Investment: project initiation of new technologies.
2. Technology learning and adaptation.
3. Rationalization: management control.
4. Maturity: widespread technology transfer.

The phases at this point are conceptual and intuitive. They cannot be readily measured and it is not always readily apparent when we move from one phase to the next.

The first phase is characterized by an organization's attempt to introduce some new information technology. This typically requires the planning and initiation of one or more systems development projects. It can also produce major training efforts involving the MIS staff and one or more user departments. The possibility of a complete failure is inherent in the uncertain estimates of costs and benefits. The duration of projects in this category may extend to several years. Successful completion of projects in this phase depend on a number of internal and external factors. These factors have important implications in the design of a control system. Almost any organization will have at least some projects in this phase.

The second phase involves the initial adaptation and application of the new technology within the organization. This phase also encompasses the need for learning by both users and the MIS staff. The new technology will be applied in areas that may not have been foreseen in the initial planning stages. Adjustments may have to be made because of new technological developments. Numerous refinements will be made and a high degree of flexibility will be needed. Controls must not discourage the learning, adaptation, and experimentation that is necessary for a successful transition into phase 3.

During the third phase the MIS staff and users begin to design and test, on a limited basis, controls that will eventually be in place when the new technology is implemented. Again, flexibility in instituting the controls is called for, since learning and experimentation should still be encouraged.

The fourth and final involves the introduction and application of the new technology on a company-wide basis. The controls that were developed and refined in the third phase should also be instituted on a company-wide basis.

Many interesting questions can be asked for any particular MIS application. How much time and money is to be invested in each phase? Can phases be shortened or even skipped? Will the phases for decentralized systems be similar to those experienced for traditional DP? How loose should controls be in the early phases? At this point we have no guidelines to give us answers to these questions.

From a management and especially a management control viewpoint it is important to realize that, in any given organization, important MIS technology projects may be in different phases of technology assimilation at any given time. Each phase will require planning and control procedures that take into account the characteristics of that particular phase. This means that the control system must be flexible and tailored to the specific conditions of the project involved. Control procedures applicable to one project may not be appropriate for another.

The relative importance of MISs for the organization

The relative importance of an MIS to the success of an organization varies greatly. For some organizations, a well functioning MIS will be of great strategic importance. This means that it is a critical success factor. Failure to develop and maintain a high level of performance in critical aspects of the MIS will seriously impair progress toward corporate goals and have a negative impact on the organization's competitive position. In other organizations the MIS, while playing an important supportive role in the management of the organization, will have no critical impact on the organization's success. This varying relative importance of the MIS function has, of course, important implications for the management of the MIS function. Cash, McFarlan, and McKenney distinguish four classifications of relative importance:

Strategic Here the smooth functioning of some of the existing MISs and the successful development of new systems is critical to the success and survival of the organization. Banks and other financial institutions are frequently cited as examples falling into this category. Top management attention should be given to the MIS function, especially when strategic plans are formulated, since it is of critical importance. Recent literature suggests that we include strategic information systems (SISs) under this category. The primary function of the SIS is to support or shape the competitive strategy of the organization.

Turnaround Organizations in this category may presently have satisfactory MISs, but the attainment of strategic goals may be seriously jeopardized if careful MIS planning and development do not assure that future needs are met. In other words, currently MISs are not critically important, but may become critical unless future MIS failures are avoided through careful planning and development. This planning and development requires the involvement of senior management.

Factory The MISs can function satisfactorily without a direct linkage to strategic plans in this kind of organization. Major involvement on the part of senior management is not needed. Operational and long-range MIS planning can be carried out at a lower level.

Support Here the performance of the MISs is not of critical importance.

It should be noted that the relative importance of the MIS function to an organization is not always self-evident. Generally, it requires identification of the organization's critical success factors and a careful assessment of the MIS function's potential positive or negative impact on these variables. If the present of future impact is considerable the importance of the MISs will most likely be strategic or factory. If there is no impact, the MISs only play a supporting role in the organization.

Types of MIS application

The ongoing MIS activities in an organization can be classified in yet another way. Some of the activities are concerned with what is referred to as traditional data processing; others deal with internal and external data bases; others are concerned with office support and telecommunications; and still others deal with end user computing. Each of these activities differs from the other in ways that have important implications for management planning and control. A description of these activities now follows.

Traditional data processing

Data processing includes financial accounting, cost accounting, and the entire management control system. The output of these systems is determined in advance by management or pre-specified externally. This means that the users must accept the output as it comes, usually in a fairly standardized format. DP systems essentially collect, process, classify, and summarize an organization's transactions in periodic reports. These systems are patterned after the organization's structure.

The fact that these systems are pre-specified does not mean that frequent changes are not required. Major and minor changes in these systems require the services of a professional MIS staff. Often these systems were the first in an organization to be computerized and considerable experience in dealing with them is available. Their operations may be seen as routing and the required modification does not represent a serious challenge to the MIS staff.

Designing and developing new systems may represent a major effort and require projects that may extend over several years, although new systems in this category will seldom require complete in-house programming and development, since suitable software can usually be purchased externally. There is little diffusion of technology to non-MIS staff or users. Interaction with users is limited. Effective management controls are usually in place.

Data base manage-ment

Data base management systems are software systems that may enable the user to create and update files; select and retrieve information; and generate reports. These systems can be accessed not only by applications programmers but also by large numbers of users from a number of different locations. Thus we have users interacting directly with the system. Non-MIS staff are direct users of MIS technology. This involvement usually means there is increased user participation in the design and operations of the system.

Office Automation and Tele-communi-cations

There is no uniform definition of office automation. This new application of MIS technology is still in an experimental stage. Most definitions include word processing; electronic filing; voice, image, and data communications; local area networks; and wide are communications. Some of these include access to corporate data banks. The diffusion of MIS technology goes far beyond that experienced with data banks. The number and variety of non-MIS staff involved is greater. Users will do their own systems development.

Experience in terms of planning and control is limited. The diffusion of MIS activities and hardware over organizational boundaries poses added management control problems. Among other things, this requires an effort to plan the computer architecture across the entire organization. Ways must be found to manage this dispersed MIS.

End user computing

End user computing is perhaps the most rapidly expanding MIS activity. Other terms used to describe this activity are executive support systems, decision support systems, expert systems, or professional support systems. In general, EUC covers all situations where an executive or a professional uses a personal computer in direct support of his or her work. The most frequent examples is the use of spreadsheets. The systems often include on-line queries, modeling programs, and statistical packages. In many organizations, end users have access to portions of internal and external data banks.

There is considerable overlap between end user computing and other MIS applications. As mentioned, end user computing usually has access to data bases, the results of end user computing may be processed by office support systems, and the reports generated may be communicated through electronic mail. End user computing tends to transcend organizational boundaries to a greater extent than office automation. End user systems may use parts of traditional DP, have access to corporate data banks, and use the services of the automated office. This diffusion of the activity poses challenging problems with regard to its organizational placement and managerial control. End user computing is one of the most recent important developments in the MIS area, and there exists little experience in managing this activity.

Management accountants have long recognized that the design of any management control system should be contingent on situational, technological, organizational, and environmental factors. This means that there is no universally applicable design for an effective planning and

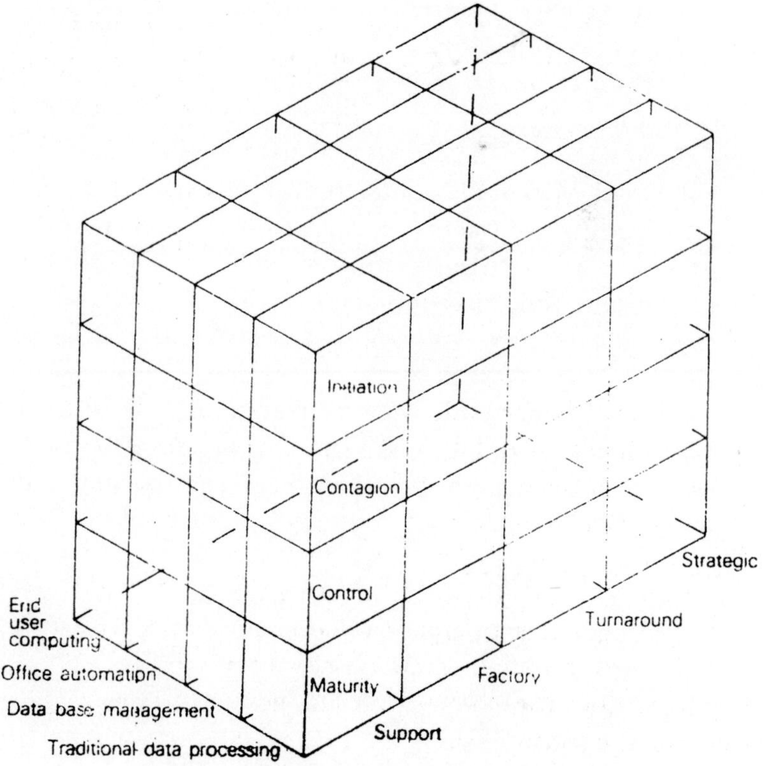

Figure 1: MIS planning and control cube

control system. Although neither the empirical nor the theoretical research in this area has produced any definitive guidelines for the design of management control systems, there is a consensus that all the relevant factors should be given careful consideration in the design and operation of a control system. In this section we shall try to systematically classify the relevant factors discussed in the preceding sections. We think that such a classification will assist in the design of appropriate management control systems and processes for MIS organizations and activities.

Figure 1 shows a three-dimensional matrix—a cube. The vertical axis represents the various phases of MIS technology assimilation from initiation to maturity. On the horizontal axis to the right we show the four classifications of the relative importance of the MIS to the organization. The horizontal axis to the left shows the different MIS applications from traditional DP to end user computing. Each cell in this 4 x 4 x 4 space represents a potentially unique set of management planning and control requirements. The categories along the three axes have some important characteristics in common. As pointed out earlier, the literature on planning and control systems frequently divides an organization's planning and control processes into three cycles: strategic planning, management control, and task control.

Strategic planning

Numerous alternatives
Environmental factors important
High degree of uncertainty
Emphasis on planning
Evaluation of performance very difficult
Long time horizon
End result: policies and programs

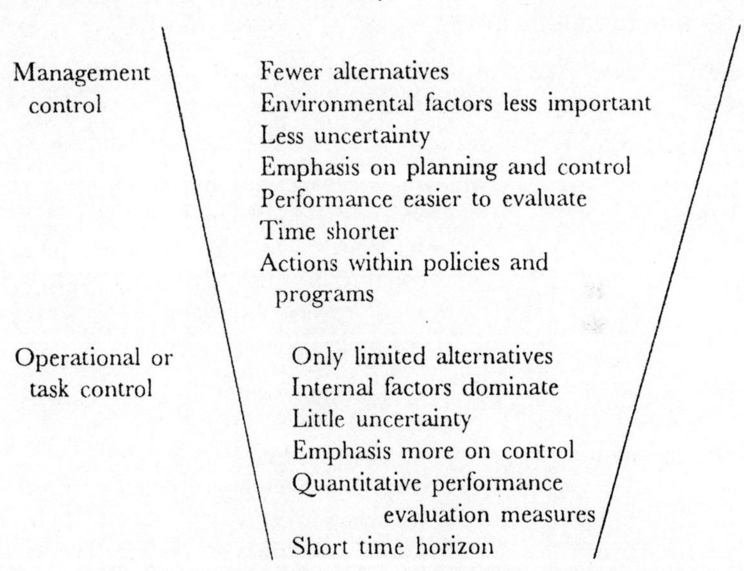

Fig. 2: Option convergence in the planning and control process

As Figure 2 shows, the number of possible actions and alternatives diminishes rapidly as we move from strategic planning to operational or task control. We can also observe that the uncertainty surrounding the outcomes of decisions decreases as we move from strategic planning to operational control. Also, decisions problems tend to become more structured as we move downwards. In simple terms we could say that at the bottom of figure we are certain as to what we want and as to what it takes to get it there. This idea of reducing uncertainty and the number of options as our plans become more concrete and specific can also be applied to MIS activities. If we look at the vertical axis representing the phases of technology assimilation, we find that during the initiation stage we are usually uncertain as to how the new technology should be initiated. Numerous alternatives are considered and some are explored experimentally. Experimentation and learning predominate in this phase.

Investment, project initiation	Uncertain as to how to technology initiate new Many alternatives, with much experience and learning taking place Uncertainty exists about development efforts and the length of the project	Phase 1
Technological learning and adaptation	Less uncertainty as to how tasks are to be accomplished Less experimentation and learning Fewer alternatives Less uncertainty of outcomes	Phase 2
Rationalization, management control	Knowledge of what needs to be accomplished Uncertain about, controls, and alternative controls may be considered	Phase 3
Maturity, widespread technology transfer	Little uncertainty Knowledge of what to do How to accomplish it Quantitative controls	Phase 4

Fig. 3: Option convergence during technology assimilation

As we move into the learning and adaptation phase the number of alternatives are limited. Experimentation and learning still take place, but within a much narrower range. In the control phase there is a very definitive idea as to what needs to be done and the emphasis is on developing effective control. These controls are in place at the maturity phase.

On the horizontal technological factors axis, we find a similar reduction of alternatives as we move from end user computing to traditional data processing. End user computing and office automation are still very much in the experimental and learning stage. The microcomputer enables end users, mainly the managerial and professionals staffs, to perform many types of analyses that had previously required paper, pencil, calculators, and information that had to be extracted from paper files. The microcomputer also lets the user perform independently many applications that had previously been performed exclusively in the DP department. The end user can now access central data banks and communicate with other computers.

These developments pose numerous management control problems and management policies are needed to cover their use. Many technological issues need to be resolved. The fact that the available technology is constantly changing further complicates the problem. Questions as to hardware and software standardization, the systematic training of staff, data security procedures, and the proper safeguards to assure the reliability of output and audit trails need to be resolved. The fact that end users are scattered over a large number of functions and departments makes the establishment and enforcement of policies even more complex. While there is an obvious need for control, care must be taken that these controls do not stifle much needed user experimentation and learning.

In office automation (OA) we not only have a diffusion of the activities over virtually the entire organization, but we are now dealing with professional and clerical staffs at varying levels of sophistication. In both end user computing and office automation, the management of most organizations have little experience in managing these functions and are therefore uncertain as to what exactly should be accomplished with the new technology.

Many organizations have considerable experience in managing data banks. This, and the fact that most data banks are developed and maintained by MIS professionals, makes management control issues less complex than in the case of end user computing and OA. These systems transcend the MIS department and significant user influence must be considered. The number of alternatives to be considered and the degree of uncertainty in regard to what is to be accomplished, however, is considerably smaller than compared with end user computing and OA. The management control problems are much simpler as we move toward traditional data processing. A large store of experience exists and there is usually little uncertainty as to what management wants to be accomplished. User input, after the initial design phase, is limited and the bulk of the activity is confined to the MIS department.

To the right on the horizontal axis, the strategic organization response axis, we find an increasing need for top management participation in MIS planning and controls. As the MIS function becomes more important to an organization, it usually supports fewer structured decisions. The need for strategic MIS planning assumes more importance as we move to turnaround and strategic systems.

Strategic MIS planning and control require the involvement of top management. The chief MIS executive must become a true participant in the strategic planning process. Only a clear understanding of the issues of an organization's strategy will enable the MIS executive to design MISs that may eventually be of vital importance to an organization's success. The need for top management's participation declines as we move from strategically important MISs to support systems.

Evaluating the performance of systems that support the strategic planning function is a very difficult task. The strategic planning activity itself is difficult to evaluate. Its success or failure can usually only be judged in the long run. There is no easy way to plan for the control of such activities. The same difficulties apply to the evaluation of systems that support such activities. Their function is to provide relevant information as defined by the managers and the staff responsible for developing corporate strategy. Generally, routine evaluations are not possible. Periodic evaluation studies could be based on such factors as user attitudes, on the quality of the resulting strategies will usually be very difficult to determine.

Management control issues and the cube

In the preceding discussion we pointed out that the design of an effective control system is contingent on a number of factors. Identification of the relevant factors is possible only when the designer of the control system has a thorough understanding of the activity and its objectives. The examples presented have shown that MIS activities vary greatly in terms of their complexity and the uncertainty that surrounds them. The greater the complexity and the uncertainty the more difficult it will be to identify all relevant factors.

Organizations react to growing uncertainty by increasing differentiation and specialization. Complex tasks are broken up into components which are assigned to different specialists. Much more effort is devoted to planning complex activities with uncertain outcomes than to simple activities. Controls applicable in complex uncertain situations differ from controls in simple situations

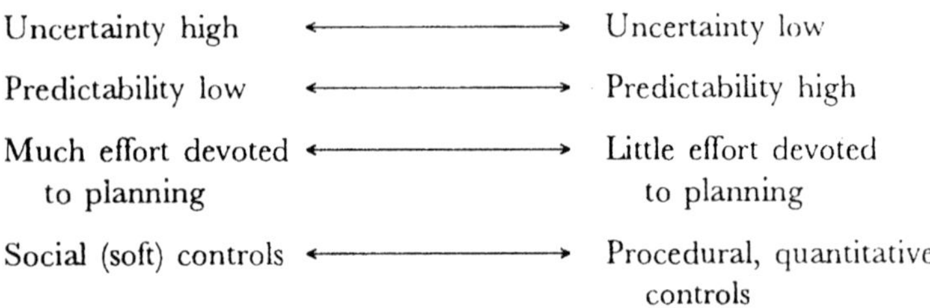

Fig. 4: Task complexity and control spectrum

The organizational structure and the controls of the traditional DP shop reflect this differentiation by segregating systems design and development functions from the routine activities concerned with running the CPU. Management controls in these two departments are usually quite different. Controls for running of the CPU are highly procedural. Exactly what needs to be done and when to do it is known. Planning for the activity is therefore simple and does not require much effort. We can prescribe exact procedures and evaluate their execution with quantitative measures or standards.

Experimenting with various hardware configurations and design alternatives for a new data base management application system is a complex task. Uncertainty exists as to what and as to when. Exact procedural controls are not appropriate and other less rigid (social or self) controls, such as peer reviews, must be developed. For example, end users could be induced to standardize hardware and software by establishing a policy that the MIS department will maintain only certain brands of PCs, that free training will be provided for only standardized software, and that sizeable discounts will be available for machines bought through the company's centralized purchasing unit.

Between these extremes appropriate controls will probably be a combination of both kinds of controls. There are no simple standardized approaches for developing sound controls. The number of factors and the relative importance of factors to be considered will vary for each situation. What we propose is a systematic approach for identifying the relevant factors with the help of the cube. Once these factors are identified we can proceed with the design of an appropriate planning and control system. The same approach may be applied to the evaluation of existing control systems.

We suggest that the following steps be taken whenever new planning and control systems need to be designed. They should also be applied when there is a need to evaluate or modify existing systems (planning a major systems development project, creation of a new department within the MIS organization, or the review of existing planning and control procedures).

1. Locate the position of the project or department on each axis of the cube. This identifies the mini cubes representing the project or department under consideration.

2. Identify and list the factors within the position of each axis. Figures should prove helpful in doing this.
3. Define the goals of your management control system.
4. Design the details of the system. This includes the careful scrutiny of project plans, identification of key activities and their timetable, assessment of uncertainties of goal attainment for each activity, identification of the resources assigned to each activity, and a decision as to what controls are appropriate for the overall project and its components.

It is important to realize that the controls thus established are not of a permanent nature. Even within projects, controls appropriate in the early stages may need to be changed as the project nears its completion. The relevant control factors of the entire project will change significantly as we move from initiation to maturity or as the relative importance to the organization changes, say, from factory to strategic. Failure to change a control system when needed may lead to dysfunctional actions. Periodic reviews of the control systems should help alleviate this problem. To demonstrate the application of the multidimensional approach described in the previous sections we present some common MIS control problems. To provide continuity across examples in the same environment, a large banking operation with several subsidiary banks will be used. It will be assumed that significant computing activities already exist at each bank in the system. Thus, each bank has its own set of MIS resources and tasks. It should be pointed out that all of the following four examples could be occurring at the same time.

The personnel management system at one of the banks in the system is currently maintained manually. Complete dossiers are kept on all employees and are stored in locked file cabinets. Two individuals are involved in the management of the personnel files: the personnel director and one clerk. Because the turnover at the bank is low, employee records are created or deleted only three or four times a month. The entire file is updated twice a year for performance evaluation and promotion purposes, but even then there are only 200 employees.

The only processing problem that exists in the manual personnel system lies in the reporting function. Government regulations on employment policies require many reports on the bank's personnel activities. The volume is not necessarily high, but there is no common format to these reports. Also, internal bank manager occasionally request performance reports on only their employees on an ad hoc basis.

To facilitate these reporting tasks a computer-based personnel system is planned. Only a single personnel file would need to be maintained on the bank's mainframe. Updating employee records and the periodic performance evaluations will be done on a batch basis. Even the OEO and ad hoc bank reports can be done on a batch basis. Data entry and processing would be done at the bank's central DP department, so the impact on the personnel department would be minimal.

As figure 5 shows, this represents the safest application. From a technological perspective, the system is very structured. The design of the application has been essentially fixed by the design of the manual system and the cost savings are easily determined. From an organizational importance perspective this is clearly a support function. Although this is a new application, from the user's view there is little difference in the organization's learning perspective. The same data are collected and put on paper, only now the paper is a coding sheet for the DP department; and the content of the reports is the same, only now it is generated on a computer. Little or no experimentation is expected.

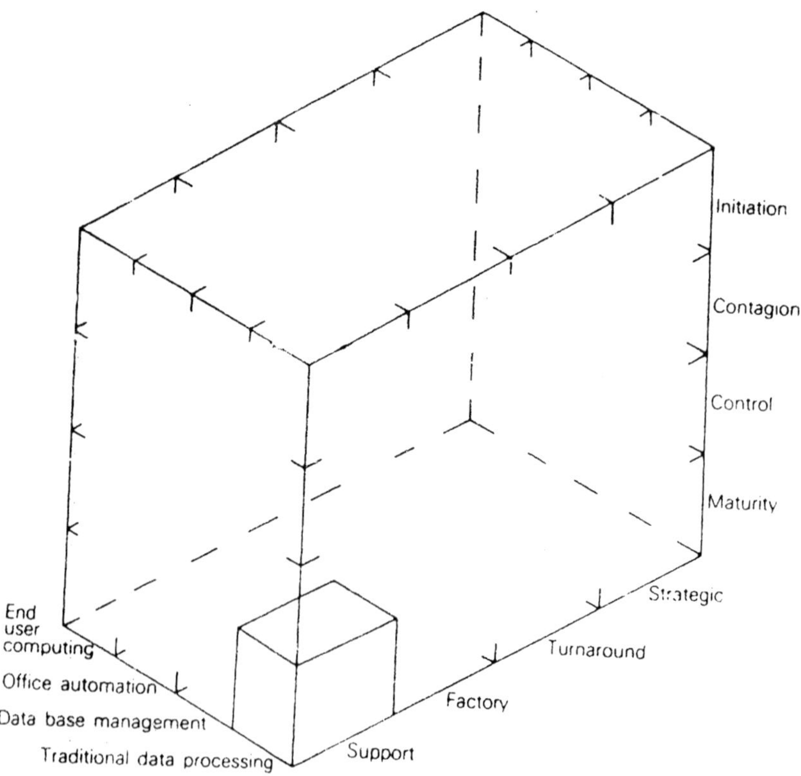

Fig. 5: Computerization of a manual system

This application can be very well controlled. The benefits can easily be quantified. The design requirements are already determined and very structured, so that the programming and implementation effort can be readily estimated. The operating needs are also well defined so that operating costs can be accurately forecasted. The MCS would consist of engineered, programming, and operating costs; tight control of time and expense budgets; and the use of quantitative measures of performance. Little variation from budget would be expected.

A strategic planning system for the President

The bank president would like a system to evaluate both the current and future market positions of the bank. The criteria for evaluation will obviously include some internal financial data, but they will also include many external financial measures of the economy and the competition, demographic data of their customer base, and qualitative assessments of new customer services. A complete list of the criteria is not known at this time and will probably change very rapidly. How each of these criteria will impact the president's decision making is unclear, even to the bank president. And finally, because of the highly competitive nature of the banking industry, the president needs to have complete control over the entire system: data entry, processing, and reporting.

A consulting firm is to be hired to build the system. Lotus 1-2-3 will be used and an IBM/PC AT is the hardware of choice. Spreadsheets including the initial set of criteria will be constructed and tested by the consulting firm. The president will also have personal training in the use of a PC and the Lotus 1-2-3 program. The hardware will be housed in the president's office with the keyboard under lock and key.

The type of system lies farthest from the origin in the cube. The direct involvement of the user in the system places it in the end user computing level of technology. Because such a system has been attempted before, the criteria for its success are undefined and significant learning and experimentation will have to take place; it would be considered in the initiation stage. The intended purpose of the system (seeking new competitive markets), and the uncertain outcome of efforts, define this system as strategic.

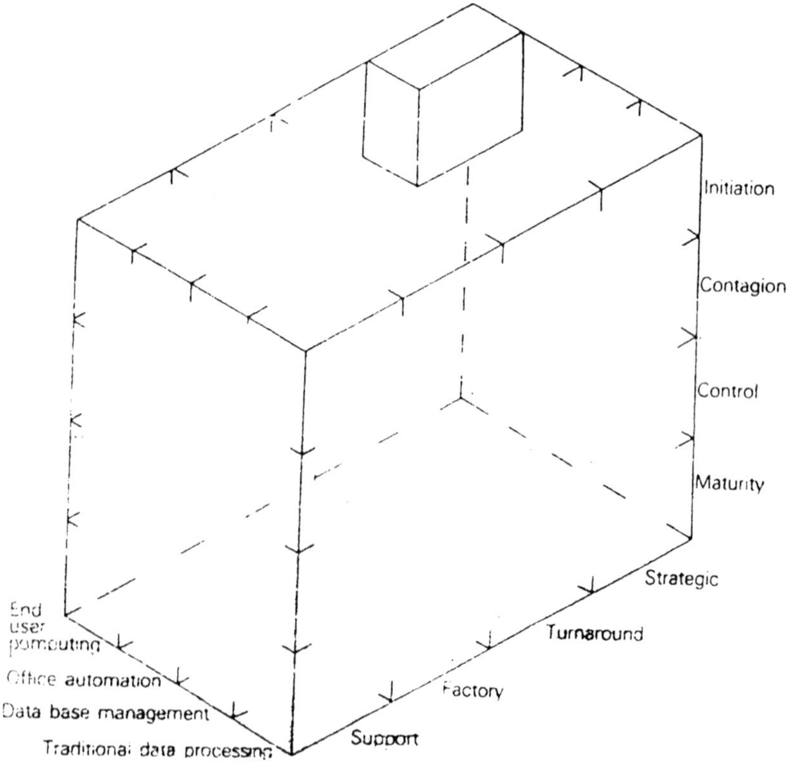

Fig. 6: A strategic planning system for the president

What type of MCS applies here? The one-time development and purchasing costs are easily quantifiable. The operating costs, that is the cost of the time that the blank president spends on using the system, are hard to determine.

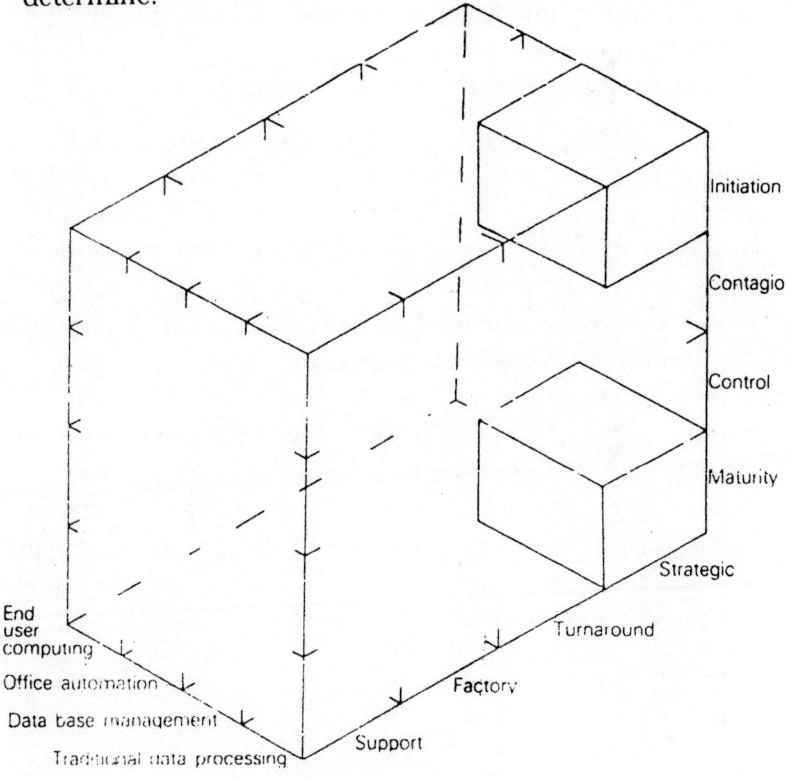

Fig. 7: Standardization of MIS functions

Even if one could calculate the opportunity cost of the time spent, how could one determine the value of this time spent? One would not want to impose a limit of five hours a week on the bank president and run the chance of missing a potential new market. Also, how can one evaluate the president's decisions, with or without the system? The impact of strategic decisions may not be felt for several years. Thus, the MCS would involve the subjective evaluation by the bank president on the costs and benefits of the system. An overall performance evaluation of a strategic planning system will require a special study, taking into account such factors as user attitudes, value perception, information usage, and possibly the decision performance by its users.

The vice-president for operations wants to offer a new service to the bank's corporate clients. A dial-in facility would be provided where customer with large amounts of cash flowing through the bank on a daily basis could get expert advice on how best to invest their cash. A cash management expert would sit at the end of the bank's hookup. This individual would be sitting in front of a terminal that would give him access to the client's current account balances in addition to current market activity. The system would also have spreadsheet capabilities so that the expert could evaluate "what-if" situations for the client while still on the phone. Once an action was agreed upon, the bank analyst could initiate the paperwork required to formalize the transaction.

7

INFORMATION TECHNOLOGY: A STRATEGIC RESOURCE

IT is becoming a strategic resource. As we look at the capabilities of IT it is continually increasing and the political, social, and economic context of its use is undergoing simultaneous radical changes. This combination of contextual forces for change and technological advance has created considerable rhetoric, if not 'hype', about the strategic potential of IT. Academics,consultants and practitioners are constantly searching for the latest exemplar application of IT which has yielded competitive advantage.

IT can be used strategically in at least four different ways:

1. to gain competitive advantage,
2. to improve productivity and performance,
3. to facilitate new ways of managing and organizing,
4. to develop new businesses

Of course, the boundaries between these uses are imprecise and the categories overlap, but they each represent different intents. However it could be claimed that computing, DP, IS, etc. have always been pursuing such goals. The difference is that the multiplication and convergence of information technologies provide more potential and the structural changes in economies, industries, and organizations more opportunities. Thus, a new breed of information systems—strategic information systems—has arrived. New systems pyramids represent this phenomenon as illustrated in Figure 1.

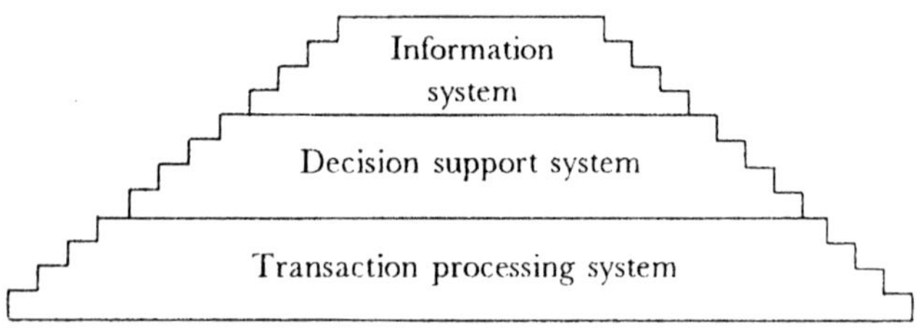

Fig.: 1 The information systems pyramid

A strategic information system supports or facilitates a particular business strategy. To a degree, an information system may be strategic only in the eye of the beholder since, one can envisage a decision support system being used as a strategic tool, or product and, however, many well known strategic information systems also would be classified as transaction processing system.

It is therefore that the strategic perspective on IT and information systems which is new.In a few years time, the concepts and practice will be quite normal. In the meantime influential articles continue demonstrating that IT can yield strategic gains and suggesting where opportunities can be found. Mostly they provide framework for analysis. None of them offers a complete answer; equally, most of them are helpful if used appropriately. Accordingly this section presents several of the well-known framework to guide users through the maze. This analysis is based on experimentation with available models and frameworks in management education, research, and consulting. Three classes of framework are proposed: awareness, opportunity, and positioning, each having its own purpose, character, and use. These three classes are subsequently sub-divided into three further sub-classes to reflect differences of analysis or approach. The implication of the framework is that a selection of frameworks best, whether for education or practical use, but that the right framework must be used for the right purpose in the right context.

Various acceptable frameworks or models of Strategic information system (SIS)

What these frameworks seems best to achieve is executive appreciation and understanding of the strategic potential and impact of IT. Awareness frameworks are more conceptual and pedagogic than prescriptive and instrumental. Extremely useful in the workshop or classroom, they hint at strategic possibilities of IT, may being to paint a vision for specific executives, firms or industries and help reorient thinking and delimit the scope. In short, their primary use turns out to be educational.

Three sub-classes of awareness frameworks may be identified;

1. refocusing frameworks which help change mind-sets.
2. impact models which suggest the scale of strategic change that may be possible, and
3. Scoping models which indicate that might be the overall strategic scope of IT for a business or sector

An early example of a refocusing framework is that of Benjamin *et al*, given below. Their strategic opportunities matrix is, like many of the frameworks, a rationalisation of recent clever uses of IT.

It is founded on two searching questions which they suggest each senior manager should ask:

- Can I use IT to make a significant change in the way we are doing business so my company can gain a competitive advantage?
- Should we, as a company, concentrate on using IT to improve our approach to the market place? Or should we centre our efforts on internal improvements in the way we currently carry out the activities of the firm?

Merrill Lynch's Cash Management Account exploited computing and telecommunications in a strategic alliance with Banc One of Ohio to create a new product market which they dominated, erect barriers to entry, and break the conventional boundaries of the financial sector. American Hospital Supply used terminal based order entry facilities in their customers to make a virtue out of a large product range and increase market share dramatically in a very competitive sector. DEC developed 'XCON", an expert system, to create computer configurations for customers, building on the knowledge of design and field service engineers. This reduced costs of rework, reduced installation delays, and thus improved both DEC's cash flow and their customers' satisfaction. It also provided a sales tool for their sales engineers. United Airlines used teleconferencing in operations management to co-ordinate across airports in emergency situations, daily briefings, and labour negotiations.

The Benjamin *et.al.* framework, by demonstration therefore, is valuable in raising executive awareness and refocusing perspectives on IT. It is less satisfactory as a searching framework for a firm because it is not specific enough by application or technology or analytical enough in terms of business strategy or management process. However it could be used to place existing IT initiatives in the firm to derive a general picture of progress.

A detailed example of an impact model is the contribution of Parsons. It is based on a recognition and analysis of the competitive environment and strategies of business and focuses on the possible opportunities of firms to exploit IT for strategic advantage. Summarized below, industry, firm and strategy levels.

Strategic Impact of IT

Level of impact	Effect of IT
Industry level	Changes fundamental nature of the industry
Fim level	Influences competitive forces facing the firm
Strategy level	Supports the generic strategy of the firm

At the industry level, Parsons points out that IT can affect the nature of an industry's products and services, the industry's markets, and/or the industry's economics of production. For example, electronic publishing, computer graphics, and communications have substantially affected the product life cycle and distribution possibilities in publishing. The power of both the technology and the information of IT have been demonstrated dramatically in the newspaper sectors.

At the firm level, Parsons draws on Porter's five competitive forces model for competitive strategy. The key message of Parsons is that IT can be used either to limit or enhance the power of rivals. competitors, suppliers, new entrants, or new products in the firm's wider competitive arena.

Parsons also borrows from Porter in his strategy level impact analysis. Here he is concerned with the positioning that successful firms adopt relative to industry structure and competitive forces. Parsons argues that IT can support each of the possible three generic strategies that Porter suggests are available to firms. These are:

1. Overall cost leadership pursuit of lowest cost production on an industry-wide basis
2. Differentiation-differentiating a product or service on an industrywide basis
3. Focus-concentration on a particular market or product niche.

Clearly many technologies can be applied to cost reduction, for example substituting robotics for labour, driving down inventory costs with stock control systems of automating effort intensive or inefficient manufacturing with CAD/CAM or process control. A packaging company sought to become the lowest cost producer in Europe. Relatively late in development of information systems it had the opportunity to explicitly align investment in IT with its lowest cost strategy. Inventory control systems to reduce working capital costs, instrumentation and process controllers to monitor and reduce inefficiencies, cost control reports to target variances, optimization models to improve throughout, and an automated warehouse to reduce stock holding costs were the main foci for investment.

Differentiation is concerned with creating uniqueness in the eyes of customers. This may be achieved through product features, customer service, added value services, technological sophistication, brand image, flexibility, quality, or customization. Both information content or technological innovation can be exploited to enhance the product or its distribution; on-line ordering, computerized quotation systems, or expert system advice are examples. An UK Insurance company, introduced FRENTEL an on-line quotation service to brokers. The objective was to differentiate in an intensely competitive market place where the leading market share does not exceed five per cent. The quotation, query, policy producing, and support facilities of FRENTEL soon earned broker loyalty in the market.

Focus strategies often combine low cost and differentiation, targeting a particular niche. The rationales vary, but technology can be used to reach special niches. Information systems can be developed to be better informed about them, and combinations of IT support of low cost and differentiation strategies can be applied when focus becomes necessary in very competitive markets. An accounting firm which was identified high value niche markets for specialist advisory services. builds databases on clients, experiences, leads and specialist knowledge all as a foundation from which they can create an image of being the unique player in that niche.

Parsons's impact framework therefore becomes a tool of persuasion. It argues that IT truly does have strategic influence. It can be tailored to a particular industry or firm to explore current trends of future potential, but at a preliminary stage of analysis. It can also be used, particularly at his strategic level, to test if current is investments in a firm are supporting its generic strategy.

Essentially, however, the strength of Parsons's framework is pedagogical to argue through whether IT is strategic.

Porter and Miller provided a useful example of a scoping model. It is not always easy to see how information can be developed and exploited for competitive advantage. Information processing concepts can be vague and we still tend to see business and industries as providers of products and occasionally services, where information is a peripheral concern. Porter and Miller's information intensity matrix brings the informations dimension to industry analysis with useful examples and can be used as preliminary assessor of overall potential for exploiting IT for strategic advantage in a particular sector. For whilst a general trend in the strategic importance of IT is evident, at the industry level the direction and pace of change differ.

The vertical dimension of the matrix measures the information intensity of the value chain, defined as the 'Company's technologically and economically distinct activities it performs to do business". The horizontal axis represents the information content in the product. The publishing industry discussed above rates high on both dimensions as would most financial services. The oil industry has high information processing in its production and distribution, but little information content in its product. The cement industry is essentially a physical, process industry producing bulk, industrial product and IT unlikely to have any dramatic impact on it. Thus we see many ememplars of strategic information systems in the finance sector, the oil and petrochemical industries striving for competitive advantage and making small but not major gains. However, as the capability of IT increases and the cost decreases, we can expect industries to move towards ever higher information content in both process and product, as the arrows in the matrix imply.

Thus awareness framework tend to have high pedagogic value in raising the vision of executives, and IT professionals, for strategic use of information technologies. They show broadly what are the possibilities afforded by IT but they are generally too high level and too descriptive to guide users to specific opportunities for strategic information systems. That is the purpose of opportunity framework.

Opportunity frameworks

These frameworks are designed explicitly to be analytical tools which lead to firm-specific strategic advantage opportunities and/or clarify business strategies in order to demonstrate options for using It strategically. They are more instrumental and practical than awareness frameworks, but do have an educational role too. In principle, however, opportunity frameworks aid the process of analytical discovery of ideas for strategic information systems probabilities to be examined further by feasibility studies.

Three sub-classes may be identified:

1. Systems analysis frameworks—which provide analytical techniques to apply across a business.
2. Application search tools—which probe the characteristics of specific application areas for good fit with the potentials of IT in general or of specific technologies.
3. Business strategy frameworks—which evaluate the business strategy context and suggest where IT has a payoff.

Systems analysis frameworks

Systems analysis frameworks which investigate the information flows, impediments, gaps, and opportunities in business processes and activities are valuable because they are not confined to any particular application area or technology. They are generic. Thus even traditional methods of systems analysis and more recent methodologies of information requirements analysis may help. However they rarely have a strategic perspective. Porter and Miller's value chain analysis is more promising as it focuses on competitiveness and the role of technology.

Value chain analysis divides a company's activities into the technologically and economically distinct activities it performs to do business. There are called value activities because they should add value for which customers are willing to pay when they buy the final product or service being supplied. A business is profitable if the value it creates exceeds the cost of performing the value activities. To gain competitive advantage over its rivals, a company must either perform these activities at a lower cost or perform them in a way that leads to differentiation and premium price.

The value chain displays nine typical activities, comprising five primary activities involved in the production, marketing, distribution, and after sales servicing of the product plus four support activities which provide the inputs and infrastructure that allow the primary activities to make place. A firm's value chain is a system of interdependent activities which are connected by linkages. Linkages exist when one activity affects another in terms of cost or effectiveness; trade-offs and optimization are sought to find the right blend to achieve competitive advantage. Also linkages require co-ordination.

One firm's value chain, of course, is embedded in the collective value chains of both suppliers and customers in the industry. This industry stream of activities is termed the 'value system' by Porter and Miller.

The scope for exploitation of IT in the value chain is four-fold, applying either technology directly, or its information processing capability, to either value activities or their linkages:

1. The technology can automate and improve the physical tasks in any activity e.g. computer controlled machine tools in assembly operations.
2. The technology can physically connect and control activities across linkages, e.g. communications links between production and distribution centres.
3. Information systems can help perform, support, or manage value activities, e.g. inventory control systems.
4. Information systems can optimize or co-ordinate activities across linkages e.g. CAD-CAM systems for computer integrated manufacturing.

Clearly these applications can be beyond the firm, in the wider value system interfacing with suppliers and customers, as well as internal. Such external possibilities include telemarketing, remote sensing of equipment breakdowns or stock outs, and ATMs.

Just mapping the film's operations and processes by the value chain technique has limited value. It provides no more than a high level checklist and possible prompt for IT applications. Nevertheless one service company which had successfully exploited IT in marketing discovered by value chain analysis that its main cost base was in procurement and began to shift its focus of IS development accordingly. The key therefore is to ascertain the cost of each activity and analyse whether there is opportunity to reduce costs or add value through IT and IS. This may highlight principal areas for attention. Secondly, the linkages then can be analysed to see if there are problems of or opportunities for coordination, integration, or optimization.

Systems analysis frameworks therefore help in 'homing in' on opportunities. They direct the analyst towards areas of promise. They cannot prescribe what particular technologies have potential, and they do not delve into the specific possibilities of highlighted application areas. Thus detailed application ideas may have to be elicited from application users and specialists or prompted by more specific frameworks such as those in the next subclass.

Applications search tools

Applications search tools focus on a specific applications area (and perhaps also on a specific technology) describing, analysing, and evaluating in detail the typical information processing requirements, attributes, or gaps. A useful example is the customer resource life cycle. This plots the life cycle of how a customer acquires a product or service and therefore focuses on the linkage between the supplying firm and its customers. The goal is to see where IS and IT can be harnessed to improve customer service, with benefits to each party. The supplier uses IT to solidify its business relationship with its customers. While the customer benefits from the added value of enhanced customer service. Incidentally, the potential value of such activities for building customer loyalty, defending market share. and creating competitive advantage often goes unnoticed Their customer resource life cycle, an earlier has taken the framework a small step further, in terms of telecommunications technology.

The major phases of the life cycle are :

1. Requirements: determining the requirements of the resource
2. Acquisition: obtaining or developing the resource
3. Stewardship: managing the resource while in inventory
4. Retirement: disposing of the resource.

Customer Resource Life Cycle

Requirements

Establish requirements how much of the resource is required? Specify requirements what are the required resource's particular attributes?

Acquisition

Select source from whom will the customer obtain the resource?

Order how will the customer order the product?

Authorize and pay for how will the customer pay for the product?

Acquire how, where and when will the customer take possession of the resource?

Test and accept how does the customer ensure the resource conforms to specifications?

Stewardship

Integrate how is the resource merged with inventory?

Monitor in what ways can the customer monitor the resource?

Upgrade how will the resource be enhanced if conditions change?

Maintain-how will the resource be repaired if it becomes necessary?

Retirement

Dispose of how will the customer move, return, sell, or dispose of the resource when it is no longer needed?

Account for how much is the customer spending on the resource?

Using Chevrolets's touch screen microcomputer system which asks showroom customers about their driving habits and type of vehicle desired and then recommends several models based on this analysis of needs, is an example of a competitive information system supporting the specific requirements step of the requirements phase of the life cycle. An estate agency provides brokers with access to an on-line mortgage search service. The system assists prospective home buyers in selecting among mortgage opportunities available through multiple sources. This is an example of a system supporting the select-a-source step of the acquisition phase. A case of a system supporting the maintain step of the stewardship phase is provided by a consumer appliance manufacturer. They provide toll free telephone access to trained repair technicians who are backed up by computer based assistance is exemplified by the hotel chains who now use IT to permit guests to check out of rooms without the time consuming process of dealing with a desk clerks.

The way to use these application examination tools is to assemble an opportunity search team of line and staff managers from the application area, together with IS specialists. In the case of the customer resource life cycle framework, those responsible for product development, product management, sales and distribution would be included. Also, customers might be involved. The team is charged with generating ideas for prospective applications. Aided by the tool, the group then critically reviews current performance and practices. considers what competitors might be doing and aims to discover new and innovative opportunities presented by either development of new systems or enhancement of existing ones. Thus applications examinations tools can be used in singular, targeted studies. However they are often given impetus by the prior use of business strategy framework.

Business strategy frameworks

Business strategy frameworks are required either to ascertain or to verify the firm's driving strategic assumptions or strategic posture. They also can begin to suggest where IT can bring advantage. Michael Porter's model in Fig 5.6 of five competitive forces has its place here. It helps executives at the level of the strategic business unit to clarify their business strategy and discuss where IT may potentially yield competitive advantage in terms of defending the firm against these forces of influencing them in its favour.

Porters model helps analysis in the following ways:

1. It focuses on industry and competitive dynamics

2. It reminds us that competition is not just about the actions of rivals.
3. It provides a simple framework which facilitates discussion and yet is based on sound principles of industrial economics.
4. It usually suggests quickly which are the one or two dominant forces to consider.

However, detailed investigation is usually required subsequently to understand the sources and nature of the significant forces, what strategic actions are possible and what industry reactions are likely. There are generalizable rules, principles, and probabilities governing strategic actions on each force. One commonly finds some of the forces interact so that in reality interactive analysis are required, followed by mixed strategic actions.

Inter-organizational systems (IOS) to combat competitive forces

Inter organizational systems by Cash and Konsynski are IT applications which link up two organisations, for example supplier and customer. This framework is more a list of example uses of IT and is not exclusive but it demonstrates many of the options.

This strategic option generator is founded on the notion of strategic thrusts. Five generic thrusts and three strategic targets are posited. The flowchart is self-explanatory. Its potential value is not only the conflation of previous framework for analysis, but the logical checklist of analytical questions it provides. Like Porter's model it therefore helps most in clarifying the firm's business strategy and suggesting the direction of the IT strategy connection. It is less likely to pinpoint specific application for development.

Opportunity frameworks generally aim to show where IT can be deployed for strategic advantage and to suggest application ideas. They vary in level of analysis and in specificity. It is likely that all three sub-classes have their contribution to make. Additional systems analysis techniques may be required to bring other strategic perspectives than cost value analysis. Certainly further application search tools are needed for different application area and technologies. Most business strategy framework reasonably well, if they help indicate the technology strategy connection.

Positioning frameworks

Positioning frameworks are best seen as tools to help executives assess the strategic importance the particular character, and the inherited situation of IT for their business. The aim is to improve executives understanding of how the information systems function and IT should be managed in their particular organization. Positioning framework therefore are concerned with assessing, developing, and improving IT capabilities specific organizations. They are not very useful in searching for opportunities for strategic information systems but they can make some contribution in raising awareness of the strategic importance of IT for a firm. They thus have value in both education and efficiency.

Typically this scaling assessment has to be done at divisional business unit level, since strategic contexts and IS histories differ within organizations. Indeed in managing IT in large organization, it is important to recognize such differences, thinking of corporate IS management in a portfolio sense rather than as common and homogeneous in all constituent businesses. It is important to note, of course, that investment in just one strategic use of IT could quickly move a firm out of one management 'scenario' into another. Equally the activities of rivals, customers suppliers, or new entrants could quickly move a firm from 'support' or 'factory' to 'turnaround' or 'strategic'. Indeed it is often sector pressures, perhaps compounded by capabilities of new technologies, which create and dynamic behind the strategic grid.

Thus, although McFarlan grid is something of a tautology—the questions and answers are similar—and although it must be applied at the right level of analysis, it can help point out not only that firms are in different strategic IT contexts but emphasize that universal management prescriptions in this field rarely make sense.

Spatial frameworks

An example of a spatial framework is Earl's sector model. This contrasts sectors from an IT perspective and leads to a more subtle framework emphasizing sector nuances in IS strategy formulation.

In some sectors, for example financial services, airlines and, increasingly, retailing. It has become the means of delivering the goods and services in the sector. Indeed the infrastructure of the sector is often IT itself and so each firm's IT infrastructure is a major plank of its asset mobile and textile manufacturing, business and functional strategies are increasingly dependent on IT for their implementation. Indeed critical success or survival factors in those industries are often reliant upon it for their achievement. This is the 'dependent' class. In a third set of sectors, management believe that IT can yield some competitive advantage and that poor IS may prove to be a competitive disadvantage. However, the requirements and imperatives are by no means clear and managements need faith in IT and IS and have to drive continually for the next benefits. This set is called 'drive', and chemical and food companies seem to fit it. For the final group of sectors, the strategic importance of IT is either not yet apparent or is minimal. IT is never irrelevant but it is unlikely to make or break company performance in these sectors. This class is called' delayed' —for technologies or competitive forces may prompt a reappraisal in the future.

This four way classification is given below. Management differences might include the following: in delivery sectors, technology policies are important, investment IT is continuous and business strategy and IT strategy are very closely inter-weaved. In dependent sectors, business-led direction is crucial, evaluation of IT can be against clear goals and strategies for IT and IS must be a function of business strategies. In drive sectors, users need to lead the use of IT as much as do IT managers, experiments and risks are to be encouraged, and spotting and recognizing winning applications is key. In delayed sectors, the profile of information management need not be high, much activity can be left to the specialists, and investment in IT is limited.

Again, the condition of sectors can change over time. Cumulative dependence on IT can render a dependent sector firm eventually like a delivery sector firm and certainly a spectacular strategic strike by a firm in a drive sector may change the industry and thus its classification.

The main value of this framework is in thinking about sectors in an IT perspective rather than through more traditional lenses. Then the approach demanded on management can be explored. For example it becomes apparent that in delivery sectors, management are 'stuck with IT. If they thought 'it might go away soon', they have to revise their ideas. For managements in dependent sectors, who often worry that 'they are not like banks or airlines', they begin to see that whilst IT has an important place it is up to them to put it in its appropriate place—and not leave too much to the specialists.

Temporal frameworks

Temporal frameworks are concerned with historiographies of IT. The classical model is Gibson and Nolan's stages of EDP growth which suggested that firms move through four stages of learning how to manage EDP. Learning was seen to be through experience and each set of management practices in a stage was function of events in the last stage and anticipated needs in the next. This framework, which has been subjected to empirical testing, has become controversial, but it is by no means clear that the general trend is invalid and certainly most managers identify with it very readily. Some workers have developed or seen tools based on this framework as one set of IS strategy methodologies emerge some interesting tensions assess a firm's IT management experience through this framework and then compare the agreed positioning with the metaphor chosen when McFarlan *et al's* strategic grid was applied.

The most generalizable temporal framework is the technology assimilation model of McFarlan and McKenney which can be applied to any particular information technology or perhaps to the average condition across IT as a whole stage one. The emphasis is on trying out a technology and management stage one, the emphasis is on trying out a technology and management planning and control is thus relatively lax. In stage two, the emphasis is on expanding technology use so that management by exhortation and enthusiasm is likely. In stage three, concerns over cost, reliability and user satisfaction lead to introduction of management controls. In stage four, managements, users, and specialists begin to feel comfortable about the uses, supply, and implications of the technology and a more balanced management approach evolves.

Commonly, organizations place themselves in late stage three for data processing. This positioning can be disastrous for organizations who also place themselves in turnaround on the strategic grid—for heavy control will not lead to stepped changes in use, innovation, or adaptation through IT. Likewise telecommunications is often placed in stage two—but if communications networks are a core part of the IT infrastructure for companies in the strategic or turnaround quadrants of the strategic grid, some rapid management evolution along the stages curves will be necessary.

So the principal use of positioning frameworks is to help managements understand the importance of IT for their firm and examine the appropriate management approaches required. Each of the three sub-classes has its values—and their benefits tend to be enhanced, if they are used in conjunction with each other. Also it can be important to time—for technology, experience, and competitive forces render them dynamic over time.

The 3 important questions for management are:

1. Why is IT important and how important is it for our firm?

2. What strategic opportunities might we seek or gain from IT?

3. Given the answers to the above two questions, should we be managing IT differently?

We find this forms a progressive process which can be looked at through the lenses of organizational development. The process behind one is that of unfreezing current management attitudes and beliefs. The task is to open up new visions or horizons and exploit current issues and discontents, the objective being to generate a healthy mix of interest and discomfort. The process behind the second question is changing managers' thinking, perhaps by discovering new emphasis, thrusts or opportunities. The task is to develop the new visions and examine the discomforts, facilitating the group to embrace new goals, consider relevant strategies and adopt changed thinking. Finally, question three is about reassessing management practices for this new thinking—about freezing again. The task here is to help the group agreed what is required to put new ideas into action, provide realistic guidance and forge common language and frameworks which will underpin further activity. So the concluding view of the framework of frameworks is one of the organizational development. We find that several awareness frameworks are needed for unfreeezing. The systems analysis, applications search, and business strategy versions of the opportunity frameworks are all required in the change phase, usually employed in workshop mode.

Framework of framework : OD perspective

Question	Development process	Framework
IT importance	Unfreeze	Awareness
IT opportunities	Change	Opportunity
IT management	Freeze	Positioning

This organizational development view therefore is consistent with the general message of this paper. Many strategic IT frameworks are useful both in demonstrating that IT is becoming a strategic resource and in suggesting how IT can be exploited and managed strategically. It is important however to understand the comparative aims and advantages of each of these models and frameworks, the framework of frameworks in this chapter seeks to help this understanding, then users can select the framework to fit the purpose, but recognizing that several frameworks are probably required. What has been left unsaid until now, however, is that whilst all these frameworks—awareness, opportunity, and positioning—provide useful early guidance in their respective areas, they provide but a start. Nearly always much detailed analysis and reasoning has to follow both in discovering strategic information systems and in modifying current management approaches to be more strategic. However, without the frameworks, managements may never understand the strategic era of IT or begin to contribute to its evolution.

Strategic information systems and organizations

It has been shown that information systems have gradually developed from stand-alone tools for improving the efficiency of individual operations to integrated systems providing support for fostering competitive advantage. To accommodate such changing roles of information systems, not only must systems reflect a company's strategic development and intent, organizational structure and work processes must also be altered or remodelled. This supplement examines approaches to managing SIS to reflect the strategic development of the company, as well as the impacts that

SIS would have on company organization and, correspondingly, work design and systems.

Information systems and organization structure

In the 1950s, when computers were first introduced for commercial use, they were applied in processing accounting data, the computer—then referred to as an electronic accounting machine—was usually located in the offices of accounting divisions.

By the 1960s in the USA and early 1970s in Japan, the growing power of computers with the advent of mainframes permitted them to perform a broader array of applications. In this period, computer and information systems tended to be large and aimed at centralizing corporate data to supply up-to-date information to senior management for decision-making or other organizational uses. The function was referred to as electronic data processing (EDP) and usually a separate division manned solely by computer personnel was created for performing such functions.

By the late 1970s and early 1980s, when the development of expert systems and decision support systems tended to strengthen the heretofore centralized function of data processing and to improve and speed up the decision-making process, small microcomputers were increasingly employed directly by various departments. This trend of dispersion and decentralization was further enhanced by the increasing availability of ready-made software packages. The result of such developments was that many departments such as marketing and finance began to instal their own microcomputers, hence thus enhancing office productivity in which microcomputers are a major tool.

As the installation of microcomputers began to proliferate they were linked into networks connected to large, centralized mainframes.Instead of being isolated, information systems became more integrated, on-line, and interactive in nature and involved in the minute-to-minute operations and decision-making processes of the company. Information systems at this stage become a core part of business operations. They can improve the decision-making process (in terms of speed, accuracy, and comprehensiveness of data), serve higher customer and client expectations, and coordinate the tasks of different departments. SIS refers to systems that directly foster strategic advantage against business rivals.

8

Information Systems and Strategic Management Integration

Given the competitive pressures in the business environment, it is imperative for companies to understand that information systems can be used as a tool to gain competitive advantage. This is a new issue facing management today, since prior to the 1980s, information systems were not a major consideration in the strategic planning of business. In essence, before identifying strategic targets for information systems, one must establish the broad strategy of a company.

In establishing corporate strategy, three basic generic strategies were suggested by Michael Porter in 1980. These are: cost leadership, market or product differentiation, and focus. Consideration of these generic strategies is helpful in understanding where strategic opportunities exist. However, in identifying where information systems can be applied, these could be based on the analytical framework of F. Warren McFarlan which was based on the competitive model of Porter and Miller, or perhaps the value chain model of Porter proposed in 1985. According to McFarlan, the specific questions to be asked in identifying areas where information systems could be applied strategically are, for example, whether the information system can build entry barriers: switch costs to customers: change the basis of competition, change the balance of power in suppliers relationship; or generate new products or services. The value chain mode, on the other hand, can be used by going through each of the nine generic activities and asking if new developments in information system can help promote new applications for one or several of these activities taken together.

Once specific projects have been identified within the overall context of the company's strategic plan, an SIS plan can be developed. An important part of this plan is the management strategy for moving from the current position to the future one. This includes such decisions as hardware acquisition, software system development, and required changes in organizational structure, work systems, and work processes.

Rise of chief information officers

As the application of information systems expands in determining the company's competitiveness and as the amount of capital required for investing in information systems escalates, it becomes necessary for senior management to plan and manage information systems as a corporate resource. This gives rise to a new category of senior management staff, the Chief Information Officer (CIO), a term first used in 1981 by W.R. Synnott, former Vice-President of the Boston Bank. The definition and tasks of a CIO, according to Synnott, is a senior staff member of the company who presides over the company's investment in information systems for the objective of strengthening both long-term and company-wide competitive strength. The main responsibility of a CIO, he said, is to work directly under the president to construct and maintain a high-quality company-wide information system architecture and to cultivate corporate understanding and vision among senior staff for achieving higher productivity, better decision- making, and stronger competitive strength through information systems. In terms of company operations, a CIO must ensure compatibility and integrity among information systems used by different departments and to train the requisite professional staff to handle the tasks.

Business Week, in an article published in 1986, cited three major roles of CIO: 1) to supervise company-wide data management, office automation systems, and technical aspects of communication with remote areas; 2) to report to senior management, such as Chief Executive Officer (CEO) or president of the corporation; and 3) to participate actively in the formulation of the corporation's long-term policies and planning while delegating the daily management task of the computer division to subordinates. With all these roles and responsibilities, it is self-evident that the calibre of the CIO should not be lower than that of corporate vice-president. This is because the roles of a CIO are identifying and designing new strategic applications and training new users, all of which require cooperation and coordination from various departments, in addition to the data-processing department which is usually under his supervision.

In pioneering the strategic use of information systems for business competition, the CIO system initially appeared in the USA. One early CIO in the USA was John Reed of Citicorp, who introduced the concept of ATMs to Citicorp and tried hard to persuade management to pursue the opportunity. The bank's first ATM was put into operation in New York in 1977. However, the initial response from customers was not encouraging and the huge amount of investment required for ATM installation diminished the profitability of the bank, especially in 1980 and 1981. John Reed pursued his visionary idea despite the difficulties, and with support from senior management the Citicorp ATM finally helped to define a new era of electronic banking.

The recognition of the importance of adequate attention from senior management to identify and manage the opportunities offered by information systems seems to be stronger in the USA than in Japan. A survey of the Information Management Association (Figure 5.12) in 1988 indicated that 20.9% of U.S. firms interviewed said that the CIO system existed in their companies (as against 3.1% in Japanese firms). The survey also revealed that 40.7% of U.S. firms interviewed said that although the CIO system did not exist in their firms, the function, in substance, did. (The corresponding figure for Japanese firms was 27.6%). Furthermore, the rank of such staff who assume the responsibility of CIO in Japanese companies, whether they carry the title of CIO or otherwise, were: presidents (13.1%). vice presidents (10.9%), senior managing directors (13.1%), managing directors (31.8%), directors (23.0%), and divisional managers (6.5%).

In Japan, some famous CIOs are Shotara Watanabe (executive vice-president of Kao Corporation), Koji Miyauchi (managing director of Yamato Transport), and Masao Hosoda (vice-president of Nippon Seiko). Many of them were in fact the propellants for the formation of the CIO Coordination Committee of Japan in 1989. The total membership of the Coordination Committee reached 100 in 1990, and all belonged to the rank of director grade or above in Japanese companies.

CIOs in Japan: Kao Corporation (Case 1)

The example of Kao Corporation explains vividly the different role of being a CIO and the head of an electronic data processing or information system division. Liaising with the Management Committee and Senior Managing Directors Committee, the CIO of Kao Corporation, Shotaro Walanable, who was one of two executive vice-presidents in 1989, presides over all the strategic information agenda of the company (Fig 5.13) . His role is to adopt a strategic view on the utilization of information systems in order to foster company wide competitive advantage.

As the CIO Kao Corporation, apart form supervising both Kao Merchandising information Services, Ltd, and the knowledge and information Science Institute (which houses the New Echo System), he must take direct responsibility for all information system development projects of the company. These projects are usually identified through a company-wide campaign for total creative revolution (TCR), which aims to foster the participation of all staff in identifying new areas for improvement and innovation. In most development of such projects involves the cooperation and coordination of other departments, including production, marketing, sales and distribution, and personnel. Projects may try to link sales branches to factories to reduce idle inventory without causing stock shortages, or to reorganize the distribution network to reduce the number of distribution centres.

CIOs in Japan : Yamato Transport Co. Ltd (Case 2)

Yamato Transport C. Ltd is another successful example of SIS application. Starting in 1976 as a private door-to-door parcel delivery business, a field which had until then been monopolized by the Japan National Railway (JNR) and post offices under the Ministry of Posts and Telecommunications. Before launching into the parcel delivery service, the company was struggling for survival as transport company in the aftermath of the oil crises which resulted in higher fuel prices and slower economic growth. While most truck transportation companies were competing with larger trucks for larger volumes of cargo, Yamato Transport chose to model its services on the similar parcel delivery business of United Parcel Service (UPS) in the USA, which aimed to complement the problematic, US mail service at that time.

Yamato's home parcel delivery, known in Japan as *takkyubin,* is a truck transportation and delivery service supported intensively by an advanced information system. The three significant competitive points of its service area: 1) parcels and guaranteed to reach almost any destination in Japan by the next day: 2) the whereabouts of parcels can be located at any time before delivery; and 3) charges are low. All these are made possible by a nation-wide parcel pick up and delivery network. as well as the innovative use of information systems. The overall operations of Yamato Transport in 1991 involved 19,000 vehicles. 800 processing centres that serve as focal points for parcel interchange, and 39,000 employees. In 1990, a total of 448 million home delivery parcels were handled.

The major components and persons responsible for the formulation of the strategic use of information systems are : the Strategic Management Meeting: KojiMiyauchi, who is the CIO and one of the managing directors of the company; the system improvement division that supervises the system development section.

Strategic Management Meetings are held weekly and attended by the company's senior management staff and divisional managers responsible for or related to the matters to be discussed at that particular meeting. These matters may include, for example, new business services to be launched. After deciding the corporate policies of the new service, the meeting instructs related divisions to prepare a detailed plan. In this connection, the development of a new product is undertaken by the product development division, and the launch of a new sales campaign is undertaken by the business promotion division. Likewise, matters related to the development of new information systems are undertaken by the system improvement division that serves as the planning body of the company in utilizing information systems.

The responsibility of the CIO is to coordinate the efforts of the various divisions to ensure their implementation are in line with the policy decisions of the Strategic Management Committee. In 1987, joint efforts between the system improvement division and the operation improvement division resulted in the development of a wireless data transmission and collection system in order to better locate the exact position of trucks even though they are being driven along highways.

Koji Miyauchi also serves as a board member of Yamato System Development Co. Ltd., Following the basic designs and parameters of the information system determine by the system improvement division, Yamato

Development Co. Ltd. carries out the detailed development of the information system. Weekly meetings are held between the system improvement division and Yamto Development Co. Ltd. to maintain coordination. By 1989, the system improvement division had about 20 staff members and Yamato Development Co. Ltd. had about 850 staff. Furthermore, Yamato Transport held 30% of the total business volume of Yamto Development Co. Ltd., and the remaining 70% was system development for other customers.

SIS for work processors and systems

Apart from the necessity of devoting greater attention by senior management to the opportunities offered by information systems, which may lead to the appointment of a CIO in the company, the other major impacts of SIS are on the organization's work processes and systems. A 1989 survey of 31 Japanese companies and financial institutions, which were selected on the basis of their intensive use of information systems, indicates that with the introduction of SIS, most of them saw that there is necessity to give greater autonomy to operating staff to speed up decision-making processes and that horizontal communication among divisions and vertical communication along the company hierarchy were strengthened.

NSK is a typical example in this regard. General Manager Tado Ogawa of NSK's information Service Department noted that the use of an on-line CAD systems, when all the know-how for the design ball bearings, for example, is stored in the knowledge-based database, not only shortens the time required for new design but the steps formerly required for approval from the design unit all but disappear. Formerly, some two to three weeks were required to obtain the approval seals from the chief of the design unit, design section manager, and at times from design staff before replying to branch offices. With the on-line CAD system, not only do the marketing staff of the branch office become responsible for the product design, they can also check the production plans of the plants on-line to offer customers the best production scheduling. This all for greater autonomy at branch offices, speedier decision-making, and stronger horizontal communication through the information system.

In this regard, the problem of authorization must be addressed early, sometimes even before the actual implementation of an information system, in order to realize the intended benefits of the investment. Masakatsu Hosoda, formerly an NSK executive vice-president, emphasized that in parallel to the introduction of an information system, it is also important to change employees' ways of thinking and to introduce training programmes to minimize the impact of job changes and broaden the spans of responsibility. Vertical communication, on the other hand, is strengthened, as the situation of the plant can be automatically known to the board of directors or headquarters through the information system. This speeds up the pace of both operations and decision-making.

The experience of Kao Corporation also indicates a similar necessity for staff reorientation. With the introduction of advanced information system, stales, stales staff are no longer burdened with routine work such as issuing invoices and delivery instructions, and can therefore devote more time to marketing and sales promotion. Management adjustment can also be made at a much faster speed, as the latest situation at the retail end is known to management almost in real time. The emphasis on the speed of information is reflected partly in the demand by former President Murata to obtain on the first day of every month the financial statements from the preceding month. All these measures and installation demand greater autonomy for all staff to react to the rapidly changing situation and to facilitate internal communication and adjustment to new opportunities.

Information systems and competitive strategic impact

Introduction

The theoretical exploration of the strategic impacts of information systems on business management started in the early 1980s when computers began to proliferate in the business sector.This chapter recapitulates some of the discussion on the subject which, similar to the application of information systems itself, first started in the USA and later occurred in Japan. This chapter also discusses some distinctive features of SIS in Japan, as well as the different definitions of SIS adopted in the USA and Japan.

Strategic impact of SIS

Generic business competition strategies

Professor Michel Porter of Harvard University proposed in 1980 that there are three basic generic business strategies for firms to achieve success in relation to their competitors, the first, cost leadership, refers to the ability to provide comparable products or services more efficiently with the lowest outlays of capital, time, and labour by a firm. The second, market or product differentiation, refers to the ability of a firm to distinguish its products in such a way that they are of unique and superior value to customers. The third, focus, refers to the selection of a target segment in the industry and tailoring strategy to serve them to the exclusion of others. Porter further observed that in the pursuit of these strategies firms must control five competitive forces determining the industry structure within which business firms compete. These five forces are:

1) the threat of new entrants;

2) the threat of substitute products and services;

3) the bargaining power of suppliers;

4) the bargaining power of buyers; and

5) rivalry among existing competitors.

These observations, although referring to business competition in general, have set an analytical framework for subsequent discussions on the significance of SIS in strategic business management. In 1984, F. Warren McFarlan applied the analytical framework of Porter to examine the strategic impacts of information systems in business competition. In this view, information systems have moved from a strictly supporting role in the back office to one that offset new competitive opportunities. Delineating how some companies have seized opportunities while other, more complacent, ones have ended up playing the difficult game of cat-up, he recommended that executives make a competitive analysis in assessing where information systems fit in their companies to create competitive advantage. Specially, McFarlan stated the information systems can offer five strategic advantages.

1) *Building entry barriers:* Entry barriers can be formed by installing on-line networks for key customers so that

they can directly enter orders into their computers. Not only could this move be highly successful for the distributor in providing a superior service to customers but other companies would find it hard to replicate because customers may not want terminals from different distributors installed on their premises.

2) *Building switching costs for customers:* Electronic home banking is one example in this regard. When customers have learned to use such a system and have coded all monthly creditors for the system, according to McFarlan they are more reluctant to change banks than before.

3) *Changing the basis of competition:* Information systems offer opportunities for drastic cost reduction and/or to expedite the handling of rush orders. Offering such services alters the ground rules of competition in the industry.

4) *Changing the balance of power in supplier relationships:* The development of an inter-organizational system can be a powerful asset.The JIT delivery system, for example, can reduce inventory levels drastically, thus permitting significant cost savings. Similarly, computer-aided design (CAD) links from one organization to another permit faster response, smaller inventory, and better service in the final consumer.

5) *Generating new products:* The emergency of the database information service, in McFarlan's view, is the most illustrative example of new product generation. According to him, Data Resources, Inc, (DRI), the econometrics subsidiary of McGraw-Hill introduced a new product called VISILINK which permits owners of personal computers to use DRI's economics database and extract desired information.

Information system from the "value chain" perspective

In 1985, Porter and Millar incorporated the concept of the value chain into the analysis of the strategic significance of information systems. This concept, proposed earlier by Porter, divides a company's operations into nine generic activities. Among them, those operations involving the physical creation of products, marketing and delivery to customers, and after-sale services are classified as primary activities. Other operations that provide the purchase inputs, human resources, and technology development as well as general firm infrastructure such as accounting and planning which allows the primary activities to take place, are classified as supporting activities.

The profitability of a company is thus determined by the amount customers are willing to pay for the products of service less the collective cost of the company in carrying out the nine generic. To gain competitive advantage over its rivals, a company must either perform these activities at a lower cost or perform them in a way that leads to differentiation and a premium price (i.e., with more value content in the product).

According to Porter and Miller, information systems influence three areas of strategic significance when they are examined from the perspective of the value chain theory. First, the expanding capabilities of information technology and systems have offered opportunities for enhancing the efficiency and performance of each of the nine generic operations in the value chain and transforming the way their operations are performed. Taking the operation product design as an example, CAD systems are replacing many traditional design methods on the drawing boards. In production, computer-controlled industrial automation equipment is making increasing inroads on the shop floor, and even in warehousing and the procurement of parts and components computerized management information systems and on-line networking not only reduce human efforts, but offer possibilities for faster, more accurate, more flexible operations.

Second, information systems enhance a company's ability to exploit the linkages among various operations. According to Porter and Miller, although each of the nine generic operations are the building blocks of competitive advantage, the value chain is not a collection of independent operations but a system of interdependent activities that are connected by linkages. Production engineers, for example, rely on product designers to design parts that can be easily and quickly fabricated. Better components and more stringent inspection, on the other hand, can reduce the cost of after-sale service. Furthermore, linkages exist not only within a company but with suppliers and sales channels. For example, frequent supplier shipments can reduce a company's inventory needs, while appropriate packaging of suppliers products can lower handling costs. The tasks of overseeing the linkages between and among adjacent operations in the value chain are the responsibility of corporate managers. Today, according to Porter and Miller, this task of integration can be increasingly performed by using information systems though such mechanisms as networking and corporate databases.

Third, information systems expand and enhance the "competitive scope" a company physically operate. Competitive scope refers to the extent a firm can perform or coordinate subject to the constraints of product segment scope (product varieties produced and buyers company can serve), vertical scope (the extent to which the activities can be performed in-house), geographical scope (the range of regions and countries in which a firm can compete with a coordinated strategy), and industry scope (the range of related industries in which a firm can compete). Information systems, believe Porter and Miller, allow companies to coordinate value activities in far-flung geographical distances, and expand the scope in which a company can compete.

Coordinating inter operational linkages

The strategic significance of information systems in enhancing a company's capability to exploit the interlinkages among various generic business operations was further explored by John F. Rockart and James E. Short of the Massachusetts Institute of Technology's (MIT) Solan School of Management. In a paper published in 1990, they asserted that information systems today provide new approaches to one of management's oldest organisational problems, i.e. effectively managing interdependence. A firm's ability to improve continuously the effectiveness of managing interdependent operations, in their view, is the critical element in a responding to new competitive forces. In manufacturing companies, these refer to the challenge of coordinating different business activities to achieve speedy product development, better delivery, and after-sale customer support services. All of these require coordinated efforts among different activities in which information systems have an increasingly important role to play.

To speed up the process of new product development, CAD/computer-assisted manufacturing (CAM) and computer-aided engineering (CAE) equipment, for example, can provide integrated support to product designers, engineers, and material procurement and manufacturing personnel in the overall design-to-production process. The compression will lead to joint involvement by all concerned staff in the process of new product design, eliminating lengthy iterative processes (that occurred because designers did not take the needs and capabilities of other departments into account), and therefore dramatically shorten the time required.

In improving customer service, the case examples of Otis Elevator, Digital and Xerox, were cited. These companies, stated Roackart and Short, have developed service strategies and new service markets based on electronic networks, integrated databases of customer and service history, and fault signalling that goes directly from the damaged equipment to the supplier's maintenance-monitoring computer. The distinctive feature of these systems is to direct sales and service attention where it is needed, and to provide the company's design, engineering, and production personnel with direct access to fault data for improvement.

The function of product delivery can be greatly improved through information systems to integrate heretofore separate tasks such as order entry, purchasing, materials resources planning, and distribution management. Information systems are also instrumental in providing customers with information about when orders will be completed, and to manage outside suppliers, product manufacturing, and product distribution more efficiently. Information systems, asserted Rockart and Short, help exploit these linkages in order to achieve greater competitive advantage.

Information systems and strategic thrust

Wiseman noted in Strategic Information Systems that information systems affecting internal operations or tradition products and services will only have "strategic" impact if they can support the "strategic thrust" of an organization. The strategic thrust of any organization may include Porter's cost reduction and differentiation, as well as other arenas such as innovation, growth, and alliances (i.e. cooperation with other companies for joint product development, distribution etc), all of which can reinforce each other to competitive advantage. In other words, Wiseman defines SIS in a very broad sense. It can be a marketing-oriented information system, a decision support system, or a system for creating new products and services, as long as it can help foster the strategic thrust of an organisation. Wiseman called this a "practitioner approach" to define the significance of SIS.

Distinctive features of SIS in Japan

Because SIS must be developed from and closely associated with the business environment in which a company operates, SIS in Japan, while sharing many common business strategic points of significance with those in the USA, exhibits several distinctive features. First, many SIS in Japan are constructed upon the model of the JIT production system of Toyota Motors which, according to Takeshi Imai of the Information Management Association, is the basis of Japan's SIS. The frequent delivery of SEJ which is based on small-lot orders received from the respective convenience stores is a case in point of applying both an information system and the principle of JIT in the distribution and retailing sector. The rationalization of the production and distribution system of Toyo Sash, on the other hand, is an example in the manufacturing sector. The major socio-economic factors of Japan which contribute to the modelling of JIT principles in the country's SIS include: 1) the generally small size of retail stores, as in the case of SEJ convenience stores, and the seemingly contradictory need to carry a large quantity of product items in order to maintain attractiveness to customers; and 2) the strenuous efforts to reduce costs through maintaining minimum inventory, which applies to both suppliers and users, as in the case of Toyo Sash.

The second distinctive feature exhibited by many SIS in Japan is that these information systems are employed as a strategic tool to identify emerging market trends, or a means of communication with the market. This is demonstrated in the case of Maruti Department Stores, SEJ and Kao Corporation, to be described in the next chapter. The information systems of these companies are instrumental in collecting the latest market information, usually at the retailer end through the POS registry or credit cards issued. The information helps shorten the physical distance between management and the end customers, and the information collected is crucial identifying trends and for new product development. In the case of Kao Corporation, for example, all enquiries and complaints received from customers and the advice given are classified and kept in the company's database, which constitutes one major source of ideas for new product development. In other words, information systems are not conceived as a replacement for management decision-making efforts, but as a tool for the collection of the latest market information for better management decisions.

Third, while establishing barriers against rivals is one

of the main SIS features in the USA as in the case of the AHSC and the American Airlines' SABRE, in Japan information systems are employed more to strengthen already well-established business relationships. The term "locking in" customers through information systems is generally used in Japan to describe this strategy. In Japan, most retailers are clustered under large corporate groups, such as Kao Corporation and Shiseido Corporation in the fields of daily hygienic and cosmetic products, and Matsushita Electrical and Hitachi in the field of home electrical appliances. The objective of moving into computer on-line network and the installation of the POS registries at retailers is more efficient product delivery, better sales support, more rational production management, and new market identification.

Fourth, many SIS currently operating in Japan today have undergone years of incremental improvements from their very primitive origins. The development of SEJ's information system dates back to 1977 and has undergone many improvements in response to the new market environment and expansion of operations. On the other hand, the computer-integrated manufacturing (CIM) system currently operating in many Japanese factories can in fact be traced back to the various stages of factory automation (FA), CAD/CAM, and the flexible manufacturing system (FMS). Such incremental improvement efforts are associated largely with the management approach of Kaizen (literally, incessant, incremental efforts for productivity improvement) which is commonly found among Japanese enterprises.

Definition of SIS in Japan

A somewhat different definition of SIS is employed in

Japan. Takeshi Imai of the Information Management Association, Japan, defined SIS as an "information system that supports the management strategy of the firm in the provision of products and services. The information network, which is connected on-line either within the firm or with outside companies, facilitates two-way communication and hence a more organic permutation of the various business functions of sales, production, finance, and personnel administration." He explained, in addition, that locking in customers through building information systems alone cannot generate long-term competitive advantage. The success of SIS requires concerted efforts to mobilize a firm's internal resources to analyze the information collected for formulating new products and business strategies.

In other words, the definition of SIS by Takeshi Imai, while sharing many similarities with that of Porter and Wiseman, indicates that SIS are basically a means to support the strategic business thrust of a firm through cost reduction and differentiation and to help exploit interfunctional linkages. At the same time, the importance of interpreting the information collected in formulating new business strategies must be emphasized.

In differentiating SIS from general information system, Imai maintained that their distinctions can be examined from five major aspects. First, while the objective of general information systems is to improve operational efficiency, the objective of SIS is to achieve competitive advantage. Second, while general information systems are usually developed and managed by the data processing or information system division of a company. SIS is usually handled by the planning together with other divisions. Third, while the basic evaluation criteria for general information systems is benefits in cost reduction, SIS is regarded as strategic investment, and hence the risk factor must be addressed. Fourth, while the evaluation period for general information systems is short term, for SIS it is long term. Fifth, whereas the coverage of general information systems is usually internal to the company, the coverage of SIS could be both internal and external to outside companies.

Professor Kenichi Imai of Hitotsubashi University, Tokyo, also stressed the importance of understanding changing customer needs through SIS. While defining the basic role of SIS as supporting a company's competitive position, he said that such information and network systems are particularly significant in three particular areas. First, they help identify the latest market changes, which is especially important today when product life cycles are shortening and thus "real-time adjustments" are necessary. Second, SIS can promote stronger linkages of heretofore independent business operations of production, marketing, distribution, and R&D. Such linkages are essential for providing integral services to customers today who are no longer merely looking for products at the lowest prices. Third, SIS can help meet the increasingly diversified needs of customers.

The different perceptions of U.S. and Japanese companies of the roles of information systems can also be depicted by the results of a survey conducted by the Keizai Doyukai (Japan Association of Corporate Executives). The findings of the survey were published in the 1990 edition of the *White Paper on Enterprise* prepared by the association. The theme of the White Paper for the year was "Management in the Age of Information Networking." When asked about the major benefits perceived for their companies over the subsequent three years from introducing SIS, 48% of Japanese firms (as against 17% of U.S. firms) considered that SIS would be very useful for detecting market changes. Likewise, 26% of Japanese firms (as against 19% of U.S. firms) considered that information systems could facilitate new information creation through communicative networking with sub-contractors and retailers. A higher percentage of Japanese firms also believed that information systems could help enhance company-wide efficiency and interfunctional coordination.

In contrast, U.S. firms saw the more important role of SIS in establishing barriers against new entrants and in differentiating themselves from competitors. A total of 19% of U.S. firms interviewed (as against 9% of Japanese firms) said that SIS could give them superiority in establishing barriers against new entrants. On the other hand, U.S. firms saw a less significant role (than Japanese firms) for SIS in altering their bargaining power with suppliers and buyers and achieving product differentiation.

Interpreting the survey findings, the White Paper highlighted that in Japan, the construction of SIS started with the objective of pursuing intracompany rationalization and efficiency. This was then followed by the extension of networks to sub-contractors, related companies, and suppliers. The communication patterns of these networks are usually two-way and aim at the creation of new information and values, and hence new business strategies.

9

Concepts of Information Systems

This chapter, sets the stage for introducing the concepts of information systems to you. The interplay of information systems with the world of business and how increasingly information systems are becoming critical corporate resource is highlighted here. Towards the end of this chapter we briefly explore the interaction of information systems and society at large.

Information, for the modern organisation, is a resource parallel in importance to land, labour, and capital. Here, we examine the concept of information as it applies to organisations and individuals in organisations. We see how data and information are different. We look at the sources and uses of information. Communication, the process of transmitting data and information from one person or location to another is another topic. After identifying some of the internal and external sources of information, we examine how and to whom it is transmitted. We also assess the value of information. Being able to judge this value is important to any organisation. Finally, we look at information processing in perspective.

Information and data

Information is input to be acted upon, a stimulus that results in some action being taken by managers or others, or the product of some other action. Without it, an organisation is incapable of survival. In this section, we study the meaning of information and how it is different from data. Then we look at the attributes of information that should concern us when using information for managerial decision-making.

The meaning of information

What is information? There are a seemingly infinite number of definitions for this term, both in a data processing context and in common usage. Information is meaning assigned to data. For the purpose of any system or organisation, information is data that have been processed into a form that is meaningful to the recipient or user and is of real or perceived value in current or prospective decision processes. It must add to what we already know about an event or place; it must tell the recipient something that he or she did not know or could not predict. Information, in other words, adds to knowledge but must be relevant to some event, state, or process. The lack of knowledge but must be relevant to some event, state, or process. The lack of knowledge, that is, the absence of information about a particular entity, is uncertainty.

Information distinguished from data

The term information is often used imprecisely, partly because of confusion over the difference between information and data. Data (the plural of datum) are facts, records of an event that has occurred or is about to take place. Facts are independent, unrelated, and unlimited in number. For example, the items Rs 100 million sales, 10-day strike, and four pizza ovens are all data. By themselves, however, these items of data are meaningless; they must be changed to a usable form and placed in context to have value.

All data are facts, but information is not facts, even though it is based on data. Similarly, while all information originates from data, not all data may become information. Relevance is one of the key facts in distinguishing between the two. As we saw earlier, information must be relevant to a particular problem or event. Therefore, all information must be based on factual data, but only data that are relevant to the situation are information. Not all data or facts can be relevant at a given moment. Indeed some data may never be relevant to any event. For a marketing manager planning the sales program for the upcoming year, the figure of Rs 100 million in sales for the company's product X is relevant knowledge, that is, information that effects the decision-making activities. Likewise, the fact that a 10-day strike of the production personnel may occur during the first quarter is relevant information. However, the fact that the Wimpy's Restaurant just purchased four new pizza ovens is not relevant to the manager in developing a sales program.

Data become information when they undergo a transformation involving infusion with purposeful intelligence. That is information is actually data transformed so that they communicate meaning or knowledge based on data that have, through processing, been infused with intelligence, (meaning, purpose, and usefulness).

Another part of the confusion between data and information is due to the fact that what is information for one person may not be for another. In the same sense, one person's information may be data for someone else. This analogy from a manufacturing operation will demonstrate. Company A receives daily shipments of metals and chemicals from its suppliers. These materials are used to produce copper wire. Company B purchases the wire from Company A and used it to manufacture lamps and lights fixtures. The two companies operate two distinct production processes. In the first case, the raw materials include copper and the product is copper wire. In the second case, the raw materials include copper wire and the finished goods are lamps. What is a finished good for company A is actually raw material for company B.

The same relations exists between data and information. The copper wire produced by company A might be considered analogous to information. It has undergone a transformation to give it a specific value to the business. At the same time, copper wire is analogous to data (or raw material) for company B. The wire is transformed to be part of the finished product, lamps, themselves analogous to information. In each case something more—intelligence—has been added to the data of the operation to create information.

The same transformations occur all the time in the modern organisation. A cost accountant, for example, collects data on materials costs, labour costs, the hours of labour needed for a job, overhead rates, and so on, in order to develop standard product or production costs for given items. However, for someone developing contract bids, the standard costs are only one part of the larger cost package needed to develop information on break-even and profit points and levels.

The attributes of information

As we have discussed, information adds to relevant knowledge, reduces uncertainty, and supports the decision-making process in an organisation. There are, however, different kinds of information and various ways of describing an entity, object, or situation. For the moment, however, let's focus on the general attributes of information, both for an item of information and for a set of information.

The attributes of individual pieces of information are characteristics that are meaningful to the user on an item-by-item basis. That is each individual item of information can be described as to accuracy, form, frequency, breadth, origin, and time horizon.

Information processing

We have dealt quite extensively with both data and information as they apply to organisations and management. It is now evident that there is a strong relationship between data and information. Data are processed to produce information needed for decision-making and problem solving. Now we need to put the subject of using computers to produce information into proper perspective so that the reader has a better understanding of how computer systems can be effective tools to assist managers.

Organisations regularly deal with a lot of data, particularly as the result of transaction processing where important data from routine events such as ordering merchandise, controlling inventory, or giving medical treatment or diagnosis are collected, sorted, classified, summarized, and stored. Furthermore, they are used to produce reports that convey certain facts about an aspect of the business to managers and other users. The term that we assigned to these activities is transaction processing.

But there is another kind of processing, namely, information processing. Information processing is the use of a set of procedures that transform data into information needed in management. In many cases it involves using data that are stored as a result of transaction processing. However, as we have seen, information can also be drawn from sources outside the organisation.

Not all data available to a person will be needed or wanted for a specific task. For instance, a hospital administrator probably will not want or need data about the maintenance of surgical wards if the task at hand is formulating a charge policy for outpatient care in the emergency room. However, if the administrator is establishing charge policies for the use of surgery facilities, the maintenance data will be relevant and important. The point is that only selected data are processed to transform them into the needed information. Even though there is a vast resource of data available because of transaction processing, only certain items of data will be needed.

After the data are selected, the necessary processing takes place. In computer-based systems, this is performed with computer programs that carry out the calculations and manipulations to make the transformations. Access is made to different files of data and the data reduced to a manageable and relevant form—the information. Thus, information processing is data reduction, organising a high degree of detail in the data into a form that the user can work with. Processing a set of sales data, such as one containing the date, quantity, and dollar value of each individual sales order, into sales information such as total dollar sales, total item sales and sales by the product type is data reduction. Without it, managers would have a difficult time applying all of the data to the problem at hand; it would be too cumbersome and time-consuming to sift through each sales record to assimilate the needed information. As we have pointed out, computers can significantly assist managers in data reduction like this.

A major problem in information processing is delay. In both manual and computer-based processing operations, data can be processed one at a time as soon as transactions occur, or the transactions can be grouped into batches and processed later. Batching transactions thus causes delays in processing. In some cases delay will be tolerable as, for instance, when payroll data are collected on Friday and processed during the following week. But in other instances, delay is not tolerable and, in fact, immediate processing may be needed. The Strategic Air Command, which provides air protection for the United States around the clock, cannot tolerate delay in information processing when it needs to know if a certain aircraft over the country is friendly. In this case, immediate response by quick information processing is essential. Delay could be devastating.

There are many tools and techniques that can be used to help in computer-based information processing. The way in which they will be used depends on the needs of managers and organisations. But first, we need to develop a perspective on information and information processing in organisations. In the next section, we see that information is an integral part of the processes taking place within systems like organisations. The system model is our framework for examining organisations and their information gathering.

The concept of a system is that a business organisation, or more specifically, managers, place a scheme of order on the greatly varying environment in which they operate. In effect, managers try to simplify their surroundings so they can understand them and their implications. For a retail marketing manager, for example, the environment includes people, other business, the existing body of laws and regulations, different governments, competitors, and so on. The environment in this context is the set of all objects that can change or be changed by the system.

It its simplest terms, a system is a set of components that interact with one another for some purpose. It is a set of objects that are related to one another and that may be described in terms of their attributes or their component parts.

Types of systems

Systems may be abstract or physical. An abstract system is conceptual, a product of the human mind. That is, it is not a system that can be seen or pointed to as an existing entity. Examples of abstract systems include social systems, theological systems, and cultural systems. None of these entities can be photographed, drawn, or otherwise physically pictured. However, they do exist and can be discussed, studied, and analyzed.

A physical system in contrast, is a set of elements—rather than ideas or constructs—that operate in relation to each other to accomplish a common goal or purpose. Examples of physical systems include:

Computer systems: Collections of hardware elements

that work interdependently under some means of control to process data and produce outputs reports.

Communication systems: Collections of components that can represent and transmit bits of information from one point to another.

Marketing systems: Collection of people, equipment, and procedures that develop, produce, and distribute commodities, ideas and other entities to a consumer or user.

The fact that a system may be classified as abstract or physical does not imply any judgment of worth value. That is, a physical system is not more meaningful or more necessary than an abstract system. The distinction is for analytical purposes only.

System definition and element

A system is a set of components that interact with one another to accomplish a purpose or goal. Within this basic definitional framework, elements necessary for the very existence of any system may be identified. These system elements include the environment, boundaries, input/output, and components.

System environment

All systems operate within an environment. The environment surrounds the systems, both affecting and being affected by it. What we call the environment depends on the system's goals, and activities, as well as whether it is a physical or an abstract system. For example, a sociologist studying interpersonal behaviour in a social group would probably consider everyone and everything not in the group as the environment. However, a psychologist studying the personality of one group member would undoubtedly consider the other group members to be part of the environment. Similarly, a computer specialist studying the processing efficiency of the central processing unit would place the user in the environment, since he or she is not part of the CPU. However, if a computer specialist is examining the role of an organisation's computer processing system in terms of reducing operating costs and decreasing errors in handling data and information, the user would definitely be a part of the system. These examples show how different environments can be defined for systems. Further, the environment is a function of the individual who is observing or interacting with the system.

Systems boundaries: The system boundaries distinguish or separate the environment from the system. The system exists, within the boundaries, and anything lying outside them constitutes the environment. The system's boundary line determines what is included within the system and what is not.

The particular characteristic of a boundary vary according to whether a system is physical or abstract. In a physical system, the boundary is a natural line of demarcation determined by the basic system structure and the system's goals and purposes. In abstract systems, on the other hand, boundaries are typically imposed by an observer.

The arbitrary boundary line may therefore vary from observer to observer, unless everyone can agree on criteria for its selection. Under any circumstances, the abstract system's boundaries are determined by the observer's level of inquiry, the intent and purpose in drawing the line, and the observer's perceptions of the internal working of the system. In a physical system, like the central processing unit of a computer, the boundaries are fixed to contain the arithmetic/logic unit, the control unit, and the primary storage unit. However, the boundaries for an abstract system like production work group, may or may not include the foreman of the group, depending on the definition of the observer. One observer may feel the foreman is a part of the work group; another, that the foreman is outside the boundaries of the group.

Information as a corporate resource

This section propagates the view that information is a corporate resource and goes on to survey the characteristics one looks for in Computer Based Information Systems, (CBIS). It also seeks to find managerial needs for various functional activities.

An information scientist has said that, like the sun, we take Information for granted until it ceases to "shine". Another has said that whereas the power of steam was seen and harnessed. It was a century, and more, till the laws of thermodynamics were postulated. We do not propose to set the Thames on fire with earth shaking "Informatics laws" but review some well known behaviour patterns of Information.

As a corollary to Toffler's identification of the "third wave" we note that some management scientists have seen a shift in management paradigms. Of interest to us is the identification of the most important resource to be managed, "third wave" organisations : it is no surprise to see "information" getting pride of place, unseating the traditionally supreme "cash".

Profile of information

Before seeking to draw the profile of Information, it is

essential to reiterate difference between Data and Information. Data is an event, an occurrence or an action that also has historical value. Viewed from the environment and its interaction with other items of data, it becomes Information; what needs emphasis is that they are not synonymous.

Some important facets of information are as follows:

- It is highly subjective—the meaning, or interpretation of an item of occurrence depends on the recipient's slant on that event;
- It has to meet the differing needs of the various levels in the management hierarchy;
- It should possess a flexibility in the presentation of Information e.g. a bar chart is more useful than a mass of numbers;

A cynical, but often true statement, is that we do not really know what we want till we see the information presented verbally, in writing or as a display.

Desirable features in information systems (IS) are:

- It must provide information and not data that managers have to subsequently process to extract information; thus sparing the manager the pain of unnecessarily spending time on infructuous activity;
- Every change in status of the data—consequent on decisions and resultant action—must be instantaneously reflected in the data base;
- Must deliver information in formats, at desired times, to the concerned level, in the hierarchy;
- Should automatically take care of programmable decisions;

- There should be one and only one source to change the status of concerned data in the data base;
- Access to a modification of data should be capable of being governed by "need-to-know" policies.

Consequent to research by well known consultants, some canons, rules or tenets arise:

Information scientists have arrived at a very interesting finding. Component units at any level in the hierarchy will have access to 80% of its data of interest within itself and hence it only goes out to other echelons for the other 20%. This has led to the concept of Local Area Networks (LAN) and Wide Area Networks (WAN) in the interconnection of segments of the organisation. It further hypothesises that 40% would be at call of the manager's terminal without having access to other data bases.

Investigators have seen the volume of "Communicating" in the average organisation. Over 50% of a worker's time—be he a manager or whatever—is spent on handling information irrespective of mode viz speech, data, text etc. Integrating, through use of digitizing, would be highly beneficial.

Harnessing information

This section will not take on the "analysis and system design" aspects that are dealt with elsewhere. Rather we are looking at the philosophy of infusing IT into the organisation. These can be further classified into—policy, method and *modus operandi* as discussed below:

Policy of approach: There is a trichotomy: Centralised, decentralised and distributed as discussed below:

It is decided to have one computer serving the needs of the whole organisation; a hang over of the early days when computers were thought to cost a lot of money and managers fought shy of investing money on many computers.

(a) Advantages:

— Good control of all resources used—equipment, space, people etc.; and optimal utilisation;

— One policy, hence, better systems, standards, monitoring etc. will result;

— There is an economy of scale;

— Corporate level information is of high standards;

— Incorporation of new trends, techniques, add-ons etc. are easy;

— Will attract "quality" staff.

(b) Disadvantages:

— End user made distant; it-is-somewhere-in-the-company-and-not-my-system attitudes, result;

— There will be a clash of priorities;

— Turn-around times will be high, resulting in lack of faith;

— System "down" would have cataclysmal aftermath; the famous all-eggs-in-one-basket syndrome;

— The "computer culture" is retarded;

— Almost negligible co-operation from the end users who do not see it as "their" system;

— MIS will be just another management aid remaining the toy of the professional, in the view of managers;

— The manager-in-charge acquires an undue importance, resented by other users.

Decentralised—The concept that anyone that wants it, gets a computer, which arrived with the microcomputer, and reinforced with the PC explosion that has changed CBIS all over the world.

(a) Advantages

The manager sees the computer as his/hers and therefore:

- end user motivation is very high;
- there is an urge to participate in IS building;
- controls are stronger;
- priority contention does not exist;
- extra capacity available;
- responses are to suit management needs;
- meets the 80% rule adequately.

(b) Disadvantages

— There will be duplication and even triplication of effort and so sub-optimal use of the computing power;

— Information as sluggish as in manual systems; as said by a management specialist, "the garbage only gets churned out faster";

— bound to be incompatibility in systems, equipment etc.;

— Information ceases to be a "corporate" entity and the management will lose out on the benefits of the computer as a tool;

— there would be a dilution of specialist personnel;

— overall, would be an expensive policy as expressed by a cynic "it is not only dispersed computing but also dispersed systems and people; increases cost and breeds incompetence".

Distributed—Distributed data processing (DDP) is a progeny of the Microcomputer and the Communications field. It may also be seen as the culmination of many developments:

— systems approach of the late 60s:

— cheap computing, harbinger of which was the Integrated Chip (IC);

— the 80 : 20 rule emergence and awareness of it;

— digital communications:

This last policy is a good mix of all the advantages of the other two and eliminates many disadvantages.

Method—This can also be seen as a trichotomy of methodology of data manipulation: batch; interactive; online.

Batch—All transactions are collected, the master files updated on set dates and outputs to management generated on predetermined schedules. The various advantages and disadvantages can be easily catalogued.

Disadvantages worth highlighting are as follows

— There is a high degree of manual intervention involved, such as keeping a tag on transaction tiles, mounting programs, media etc.; such an environment is fraught with less potential;

— errors/duplicates will need careful trace, to ensure

that they do not re-enter the system after rectification;

— all too often, there is a proliferation of unwanted reports;

— it is difficult to keep priorities in proper perspective;

— computer awareness is the first causality since users tend to lose interest by the remoteness resulting from this mode.

Interactive—The first development to put the user in contact with the system, in which transactions are entered through terminals and all "off-line" work is shut down. A high degree of data discipline is necessary and the end user becomes responsible for the data updation. It requires very comprehensive verification through validation programs which will ensure that only "clean" data is accepted. Very clear procedures will have to be built in, in order to ensure that only entitled personnel would update and other such "security" measures will have to be incorporated.

On-line—Extending the above, to a global scale, so that users anywhere have access to databases through communication networks linking many computer and terminals. In this, not only are those that input data linked but also many others using data for their decisions. It is the current trend and brings with it, the need for very rigid security measures. A super-set of this mode is "real-time" systems. The term "real" will depend on the environment and the user's need for response; for example the response time for passenger reservation systems could be 5 seconds whereas, that of an Air Force Operations Systems could be much less than a second.

Modus Operandi—The exact way to develop the IS needs can be seen also as a trichotomy; integrate now or total; integrate later; systems perspective. These are briefly covered below:

Total system—The aim is to take every application in the organisation and implement all of them simultaneously. At first sight, this seems very attractive but is full of potential disaster, due to some very sound reasons:

— to complete the work of design, test etc., most medium sized organisations would need very large resource investment of people, space etc.; often these would not find favour since the management would be hard put, firstly to find them and, secondly, to absorb the task force; getting a temporary force would be impractical;

— during the interim, that would vary from three to five and more years, the management would lose the advantages of the computer as an aid to their management; needless to say getting them enthused later would be a mammoth problem;

— no system is static; hence the teams will be on a "chasing their tail" hunt and the systems developed would be sub-optimal;

— at the end of it all, if the teams survive, the MIS would be a very poor one.

Integrate later—Systems are developed haphazardly with the hope that some one, some time, will integrate them. Such artless thinking will end up with "islands" of "CBIS" with very little mutual support. There is many a professional who has ruled the day that he/she adopted this philosophy.

A system perspective approach—It is probably the most pragmatic one which also, by instinct, is the most palatable since it is a "Systems" approach. There is a two stage framework that is involved; noteworthy is the intimate partnership necessary between the management and the DP team:

— a macro level assessment of the functions, their mutual dependence, on further hierarchies, input/output interfaces;

— drawing up priorities, safeguards etc. and installing systems on a building block basis.

Information in the organisation

We have seen the various shades of information and the characteristics that it possesses. It is said to deserve as much, Business scene. So some authors talk about Information Resource Management (IRM) at par with other resource management. We have heard, from Forester for example, about the business enterprise having innumerable information channels coming up to decision-making points. The modern concept of LAN, is only to be an expected development as also the Data linkages now possible by carriers like the PTTs Telecommunication agencies etc. Where the two disciplines of communications and computers developed individually, their reliance on each other and the IC's appearance, has made the two converge to a synergism rarely seen in history.

If information is so all pervasive, it would be only logical that its role in the various classical functions of POSDCORD be examined. Before we do so it is worth looking at some well known terms like MIS and DSS.

Window to MIS

Ushering in the "Systems Approach", the sixties saw MIS as the binding force it encircles the classical functions, management aids etc. and is visualised as omnipresent.

Not that MIS is a new concept; only its computerisation and its new role, as a binding force, to every nook and corner of the organisation, is of recent origin. Some information techniques did exist, to provide information that allowed planning and control functions: the computer has added new dimensions—speed, accuracy, ability to handle a large volumes etc. and hence give managers the feasibility to consider many alternatives before a decision.

MIS also suffered from "over selling" by DP persons; this led to a degree of suspicion of the "unknown" distorting its usefulness, the accent being more on the machine and not on what it could do for management. It led to the well known consultants, McKinsey and Company, to comment in terms of achievement: "the computer revolution in the US has been out running all expectations. In terms of economic payoff on new applications it has rapidly lost momentum". Booz Allen and Hamilton, made an even more pertinent (pertinent in our underdeveloped context) comment that "modern generation equipment was being used for first generation System Design". Irrespective of all these disconcerting views, it would appear that in the not too distant future, the manager who cannot use the computer will become, organisationally, a misfit and dysfunctional. Computer literacy should be a *sine qua non*, at all levels.

MIS is made up of three elements—Management, Information and System. We will need to define each of the component parts to really understand MIS.

Management—This is too vast a subject to be undertaken as a precis but, for this chapter, it comprises the process/activities that describe what managers do in the operation of their organisation: plan (setting strategies/goals and selecting the best course from alternatives available); organise (tasks assigned to selected groups along with authority/delegation); control (through standards and assessing deviations). Decisions, in all these, is a fundamental necessity and our MIS has a major role to play.

The role of MIS in these functions are dealt with later in this chapter.

Information—As we have seen earlier, Information and Data are not synonymous; a fact that is highly relevant in our discussions.

Some characteristics have been looked at earlier in this chapter.

Systems—Simply put again, it is a set of elements put together, for a common objective. All systems are part of a larger system.

In areas like manufacturing, some high degree of integration has been achieved by automation; sub-systems have been linked together to achieve "synergism". Unfortunately, this has not happened in business organisations; particularly as it applies to integration through information exchange of sub-systems. For example, marketing, operations and finance are often on diverse paths and at cross purposes.

The systems concept of MIS is, therefore, one of the optimising the output of the organisation by connecting the operating sub-systems through the medium of Information exchange.

Objective of MIS—To provide Information for decision-making on planning, initiating, organising and controlling the operations of the sub-systems of the firm and to provide a synergistic organisation in the process.

Decision Support Systems (DSS)

Of recent origin, it is seen by some writers as the evolution from MIS. We, however, view it as one already encompassed in the term MIS since

— it supports decision-making in both structured and unstructured environments;

— supports decision-making at all levels;

— it, far from being a stand-alone concept, is woven into the fabric of the organisations;

— supports all aspects of decision-making processes;

— is made up of people, procedures, interactive systems etc.; intended to be evolutionary/adaptive and easy to use.

Thus MIS can be viewed as a superset of DSS.

DSS vs MIS—MIS has the following characteristics:

— gives reports and access to data; the latter by retrieval on data bases;

— involves structured Information flow:

— Information flow centered around specific functions like production, marketing, finance etc.;

— Transaction processing giving Information in consistent manner; time focus is retrospect;

MSM—Visualises structured tasks leading to a decision or action. The focus is on better solutions in the current environment. Use of modelling techniques.

DSS—Is generally interactive to the Manager to expedite the decision process and its communication, that could be direct or through storage.

Design criteria

— prepare models relevant to function and/or level in hierarchy;

— stand alone models for specific tasks but integrable to other models;

— efficient query languages interacting with the data base;

— effective mechanisms to extract data, for manipulation, from the data base;

— input flexibility in modification;

— desirable to have batch-interactive mode;

— follow, exactly, the changing patterns;

— be highly "user friendly".

Expected support

— allow *ad-hoc* enquiries; hence usually around DBMS packages (DBMS is covered elsewhere; but what is relevant is that the Data Base Management System aggregates the organisation's data with benefits of flexibility, uniqueness, expandability etc.);

— support financial/statistical analyses of desired data streams;

— a planning language for "what if ?" queries of managers;

— ability to invoke graphics;

— report generation to any desired format.

Objectives—The above leads to state the objectives of DSS as:

— assist organisational decision-making process;

— improve the effectiveness of such decision making;

— add value to the existing corporate data base.

Necessary elements of DSS

— Personal systems like spreadsheet, own application and the more recent electronic mail;

— Access to corporate entities like key company data, linkage to external data, forecast, budget etc.;

— Flexible presentations through menus, graphics etc.

One often hears the term Computer Based Information Systems (CBIS) which seems to cover all types of ISs; the comparison of a few is given below:

CBIS Type	Inputs	Processing
MIS	Processed transcation data, some management data management originated programmed models	Report generation,
DSS	Some Processed data management-oriented data; unique models.	Query response; management science/OR Modelling Simulation
TPS	Transaction data	Classifying, sorting, adding deleting, updating.
OAS	Appointments, documents; address lists.	Scheduling, word processing, data storage and retrieval.

Note:

a) A Transaction Process System (TPS) is an euphemism for Data Processing (DP). It can be defined a computer based system that captures, classified, stores, maintains, updates and retrieves transaction data for record keeping and for input to other CBIS.

b) An Office Automation System (OAS) is also known as the automated office; defined as a multifunction, integrated CBIS that allows many office activities to be performed in an electronic mode.

c) The relationship of these CBIS links with management hierarchy is often depicted as below; also shown are other management aids:

— Top Mgmt—DSS; part of OAS; MSM & OR;

— Mid Mgmt—MIS; part of OAS; Organisation theory;

— First lines—TPS; part of OAS; accounting;

— Clerical—based on OAS; Office work.

d) The growth is interesting to follow;

— mis 50s, DP; supporting first-line and some middle management need;

— early 60s, MIS; aid to first line and middle level;

— mid 60s; TPS; and MIS extending some support to top management;

— late 60s/early 70s, OAS;

— mid 70s; DSS introduced.

So what about information as corporate resource?

A very legitimate question that arises, in the mind of the

manager, that needs an immediate answer, after all these views projected, on Information as a corporate resource.

Fact 1: The information worker is a big chunk in the work force and even small improvements will have great impact;

Fact 2: Putting in order the 80% (of the 80 : 20 rule) information will improve efficiency as well as productivity.

Fact 3: People slow down communications. For example, the delays in our day-to-day work. Let us take the number of person, each a delay center, that are involved if a letter is to be sent from person A to B. A dictates, the secretary prepares a draft, this may go through one or more cycles of correction; the letter, as finalised, may await for a period for the person to sign; remain for further period in the pending/out tray; taken by a messenger to in/out registration; it will await documentation; it is then carried by a messenger, when free, and after delays in the carrier, goes through a registry, the PA and then to B.

The above, along with the more than adequate support to management in the areas dealt with later, make a CBIS an attractive proposition. It is the answer to management's problem and with the integration of the various modes of image, speech, data and text being digitised, will improve the Information sector of management.

Systems approach in business

It is used to utilise scientific analysis for firstly developing and managing operating systems (e.g. cash flow or personnel) and, secondly, designing Information Systems for decision-making. The basic tenet is that the system is held together by Information exchange.

The need for this and for the greater emphasis, is due to two factors that have accelerated management thinking to a system approach;

— the increased complexity of business and

— the increased complexity in management.

Complexity in business

— technological advances which presuppose a simultaneous managerial revolution consequent of the great need for Information;

— great emphasis on Research and Development;

— Product changes becoming necessary due to rapid obsolescence and the need to extract optimum ROI on products in shorter time spans;

— the information explosion; as the decision-maker, the manager is a processor of Information; to remain ahead of competition, she/he must be able to take decision based on a plethora of data, organised in the most optimal way.

Complexity in management

— Feed back: the output of the IS leads to a decision, leading to some action that corrects the output, which, in turn, leads to another decision;

— Automating/programming decisions by rules;

— Management sciences techniques like Linear Programming (LP), simulation etc.;

— The electronic computer with inherent capacity of handling voluminous data.

The manager of tomorrow will face a number of changes in physical processes and operations; the systems look is the only way to tackle it and that presupposes the availability of good, and flawless, ISs. This will be one that takes note of environmental changes, a highly reliable internal data bank and a model bank.

To arrive at this, perhaps utopian state, we see some essential ingredients;

— a systems approach to managing, to meet challenges, is implicit;

— the systems approach to Management must precede the design and use of MIS;

— it must be realised that the computer is only a component and not the MIS or the central focus of MIS;

— Management must get fully involved in design of MIS; islands of automation" or a string of DP systems.

Having said that, and before we look at the place of IS in various facets of Management, a view of Information needs, at the various levels of management is desirable.

Management, information and systems approach

The general model of managing is described below taking note that the functions of management are not performed sequentially; planning is involved in organising and control; organising is required for planning and control.

— Planning (setting objectives; perception of opportunities, problems, and alternatives surrounding the achievement of the objective; diagnosis of opportunities, analysis of objectives and selection of a course of action; design a program of action to achieve the objective);

— Directing (leadership in the organisational action required to achieve; includes communication and motivation of subordinates)

— Organising (supervision of action plan through an organisation whose task relationships are defined and understood);

— Controlling (observation and measurement of performance against standards for achieving the plan and correction of performance deviation if required; observation of significant trends within and without the Manager's activity so that goals and programs may be modified as necessary).

— Feedback (recycling of Information concerning plans, actions and progress at different stages of the management process to ensure that proper programming to achieve the objective is being met).

Note that the management process is interactive. Note also that a good Management System is a *sine qua non* for a MIS; it is only then that the Manager gets the Information needed in the form, place and time to perform a task. The management system helps to develop plans for achievement of objectives, to organise for implementing plans and to control performance so that plans and actions occur on schedule.

Computer applications in business

To repeat the cliche, it is the Information era, Toffler says, that is the hallmark of the later part of the century. Ever widening complexities have demanded Information at the finger tips of the user, be he (or she) a scientist, a manager, a clerk, a processional or any one that either works or wishes to enquire or calculate, or whatever.

Thus this subject can run to many pages of a write up and still not be able to do justice, to the versatility of CBIS.

In the event, it would be possible to only take broad areas in which computers are being used, and see the areas fit for CBIs. Since the intention is to get an insight into usage, we will "build" as business model and later list a few business and the commonly met applications.

A business model

As would be brought out later on Systems Development, one would look at a broad "road map" and break it down into progressively finer and finer detail until individual milestones are established. It would be a two way process. Business Strategy-Business Model-Business ProcessesOrganisations-MIS-Database-MIS-Organisations-Business Process-Business Model-Business Strategy-etc. (up to data base, is the top down planning and the return path up from database is the implementation).

As an example, we could take Banks, Insurance, or any activity in the manufacturing Service, Defence, or even a Scientific sector, and even, perhaps, Government. The type is unimportant; the general principles of business-process and classification, the methodology of looking at a Company's IS, to support a series of interlocking sub-systems would be very similar. We will, therefore, take the case of a company that distributes a mythical product called 'X'.

The starting point, logically, is the sales a record of sales or vouchers of movement from store: this will end by producing sales statistics and analysis in conjunction with the accounting and marketing processes:

Note that some of the sale inputs could go directly to the accounting process, e.g. in a supermarket, the use of check-out counter devices (which optically read through codes) price will result in total of purchases made, and, as a by product, the item and quantity sold to the order processing system.

Other resources are used up in operating a store (people, space, power etc.) and hence some kind of expense and time cards would also be sent to the accounting process; activity commonly called the "Sales Process"; after all "nothing begins until something is sold" is an old adage; hence we will see the sales order processing is the primary function interconnected to other processes (it could be bookings in a hotel system, the estimated patients in a hospital system etc.). The "customer demand" has to be met since that is the prime reason for being in the business; Management's aim is to give the customer the best product at the most reasonable prices, and, at the same time, ensure that the shareholders get good Return On Investment. It is the logical and basic start point of the business cycle. As the bins in the store become like Mother Hubbard's cupboard, orders have to be placed to replenish. The store will reorder goods based on many factors like turnover, lead time, economic order quantity etc. The sale order is, therefore, the basic document to set in train many other activities, starting with the order processing. The process will do many thing-errors in omission and commission and ensure order is valid before other processes are invoked.

After the store order has been vetted by the "order processing" process, it moves to the "inventory control" process, where it is weighed against the current inventory status in the warehouse (the two-way arrow indicates a query and answer status); if there is sufficient inventory, the "order-processing" process originates a "store-order picking document" for the warehouse and an "order invoice" for the retail store. Since resources are used at the warehouse, similar to the retail store, some expense and time records go to the "Accounting" process.

The "material control" and "transportation" processes are representative of the current approach of integrating the various processes through well planned basic information. For example orders and movements from the warehouse can be used to optimize warehouse space; based on each order, that show the cubic content and weight, as also the destination, loading and routing of trucks can be optimised.

A well designed inventory control process provides for automatic ordering based on many factors-customer Service, EOQ, and lead times. Orders are then screened against inventory record and when the level of a particular item reaches the reorder point, the "inventory" process directs the "purchasing" process to issue a purchase order to the concerned vendor. The vendor fills the order, ships the material to the warehouse and submits his invoice to be entered into the "account" process. This process triggers the "accounts payable" activity and the eventual reconciliation of cash points. Note that from the Materials control process, on receipt of material from trade, receipts enter the Inventory control process.

So far we have considered some basic processes. There are two connections that have been left out:

— one that connects inventory control and accounting

functions; necessary since inventory data is a requirement of accounting;

- the second is to show some important outputs of the accounting process; it is to be remembered that accounts is a "score-keeper", so to say, of all processes; it accumulates and outputs reports of the type shown (Inventory statistics, Sales statistics and PL statements) in many ways, as desired by management.

Note that although we have mentioned Product 'X', it should be apparent that these models would cover most applications, covering as they do, the Operational control and some management control activities.

The Marketing process uses the basic source data that has been collected and filed but processed in diverse ways to answer specific queries of management like— effort of promotion on sales, effect of price changes, product mix, diversification etc. One key output is the sales forecast based on historical sales movement (from accounting process) as well as on environmental/ projected external events (buying trends, economic factors, Government policy changes etc.).

The Strategic planning process is the core of the business model; all major company decisions are made here, based on reports of the accounting process (these are digested, reviewed and analysed).

It should be clear that any other model could be built around the basic model we have built. In a Manufacturing business model-six processes may be added: Engineering and Research; Production scheduling; requirements generation process; production control process; maintenance process & quality control.

Another perspective

We could view the "Business Process" as made up of the "Main stream", a "Support stream" and an "Administrative stream", the component parts of which are covered in the next sub-section. A later Sections we shall examine some characteristics within these streams.

The Main Stream : Can be said to be made up of:

(a) Sales order processing which, in turn, is built up by

- Customer billing, which, in turn,
- Order filling.
- transportation;

(b) Inventory reporting and control which, in turn, can be seen as—

- stock status reporting,
- statistical replenishment;

(c) Requirements generation, further seen as—

- gross requirements generation,
- net requirements generation;

(d) Production scheduling, consisting of—

- fabrication and assembly scheduling,
- shop loading;

(e) Production control made up of,

- performance vs plan analysis,
- variance reporting;

(f) Purchasing;

(g) Receiving;

- numerical control,
- configuration management,

(h) Quality control; - industrial engineering,

(i) Maintenance; etc - BOM generation; etc.

The Supportive stream : which can be seen to be made up of -

(a) Marketing made up of-
   - sales analysis,
   - sales forecasting,
   - sales administration,
   - advertising;

(b) Strategic planning built from-
   - econometric models,
   - market models,
   - simulation,
   - decision theory,
   - investment analysis,
   - facilities planning;

(c) Engineering and Research, consisting of -
   - design automation,
   - project control,

The Administrative stream : that can be seen to be made up of—

(a) Financial, consisting of -
   - accounts receivable;
   - accounts payable,
   - general ledger,
   - cost accounting,
   - fixed assets accounting,
   - budgeting,
   - financial Models,
   - Key-rated analyses,
   - Profit and Loss (P & L) statements;

(b) Personnel, made up of-
  - payroll
  - payroll reports
  - wage and compensation analyses;
  - (c) Legal,; etc.

Some characteristics of the "Business process"

Having sent a perspective of a typical business system, we intend to show up some typical characteristics under each component process. It is depicted in tables under each sub-division.

In the Figure 1.8 the following codes are being used, against column:

(a) B - Major Management Focus : Top-T; Middle-M; Operating-O; All-A;

(b) C - Typical Cycle;- Daily-D; Weekly-W; Monthly-M; Quarterly-Q; Annual-A;

(c) D - Form of processing -Structured-S; Unstructured-U; Highly S-H;

(d) F - Type of data : Internal-I; External-E:

(e) G - Time demand : Low-L; Medium-M; High-H;

(f) H - Transaction volume : Low-L; Light-l; Medium-M; Heavy-H;

(g) I - Typical mode of operation :- Batch-B; Direct-D; Online-O;

(h) J - Frequency of implementation : Low-L; Medium-M; High-H;

(i) K - Difficulty of implementation : Low-L; Medium-M; High-H;

(j) L - Complexity : Low-L; Medium-M; High-H

Other than business applications

It would be totally wrong to leave this chapter with the impression that computer usage is confined to Business Systems.

Number crunching

It must not be forgotten that the computer came into being in the mind of Babbage for solving mathematical problems. Only the fact that technology lagged behind conception ensured that the computer came to the world much later; and that too in the scientific community.

Let it be misunderstood, the use of number crunching would not be confined to the mathematician to solve problems. Other application can only exist if numbers can be operated on. Typical examples are:

— Weather forecasting;

— Man would not have landed on the moon if quick results were not obtainable;

— Oil exploration;

— Complex process control including nuclear plant; etc.

CAD/CAM

Computer have come to the aid of the Design activity. Some of the benefits of CAD are:

— drafting—that makes the life of the draftsman easy;

— the design that enables optimisation of space, density,

and modification easy not only in two dimensions but three;

— the ability to effect changes and see the results from any perspective etc.

The use of computers in the Manufacturing field would cover all aspects of the manufacturing activity including the Numerical control of Machines. Flexible Manufacturing Systems (FMS) CIM. etc. are other concepts in the field where the whole process is optimised.

Some of the more common terminologies used are : Computer Aided Production Engineering, Computer Aided Storage and Transportation, Computer Aided Production Planning, Computer Integrated Manufacturing etc.

Some of the basic features one would expect are:

Geometry creation

— creation of a complex drawing out of a set of primitives that will include point, lines, arcs, circles and polygons;

— identify any part of this drawing as a unit and repeat in a rectangle or a circle and arranging like bricks in a wall or teeth of a gear;

— identified units to be made to move, rotate, change scale, get mirror image etc.,

— zoom, layering, reference grading etc.,

Societal impact of information systems

Any new technology will always have its share of antagonists, who will number as many as the protagonists. It must be remembered that the Industrial revolution was on which automated the manual operations of mankind and it brought in its wake a high degree of opposition led by one Capt Ludd. The computer is viewed as one that is attempting to automate functions that are mundane and repetitive in the Information field and ultimately automate many of the applications requiring "thinking"

Managers and Computer people would do well to study the implications of the introduction of computers; particularly in developing countries, where the sceptre of unemployment raises its head.

Unemployment:

This is a major concerns of labour; there is fear that because of the introduction of computers there will be retrenchment. Their concern does not stop here but there is fear that future generations will suffer.

Management argues that far from displacing labour, there is, firstly opportunity for a new and better class of workers and, secondly, the result of higher productivity is greater employment potential.

Peter Drucker has dubbed the individuals dealing with information "knowledge workers". He says "the substitution of knowledge of manual effort as a productive resource in work is the greatest change in the history of work". He says that in 1900, out of 20 workers, 18 were manual workers but by 1965, in a vastly increased work force, out of 2-workers, 5 and only 5 were involved in manual labour—an indirect effect of introducing the computer.

Resistance to change:

It is common knowledge that change is to any individual

particularly if there is a threat, real or imagined to his position, his job or any such.

At the shop floor level, the threat is more perceptible and it is with great difficulty that organisations have been able to get the labour Unions to agree to computerisation.

It is the white collar worker who has shown the greatest resistance. Examples are galore and the student should investigate the happenings in Banks, Insurance companies in the private and public sector. It says much for the Unions that they have readily accepted computerisation where they see that the manual systems are not capable of handling volumes. We quote the example of the Inter Branch Reconciliation of Banks that, almost a decade ago went in for computerisation *as long as the computer was not in house.*

Researchers have found that the middle range manager has always viewed the computer with suspicion. His fear is based on the fact that many of the programmable decision can now be delegated to the computer and two factors are to be remembered:

— his/her importance reduces: He/she is no longer in a position to do favours; equally, they are in no position to suppress facts that could be compromising;

— there is speculation in journals that the Development of Information Systems, on the computer, the middle management cadre will shrink if not disappear altogether.

Strange as it may seem some top level executives also resent the coming of the computer into their sphere changing the way they perform their functions and changing their ways of functioning and learn complicated, new procedures whose effectiveness they question in the first place. Mixed up with this is a "fear of the unknown" since the computer is a best about which his/her generation had NO knowledge whatsoever.

What kind of modern Luddite action do we visualise?

— at the operational level, there could be subtle ways of introducing errors and generally making systems fail; to be borne in mind as security measures;

— at higher levels, is by ducking from involvement in systems and suppressing vital information parameters.

There is tremendous scope for choosing what to do on computer and what should be left to the human. This is a dilemma of all developing countries where there is fear of unemployment.

Privacy

One great fear of the person-in-the-street is what one may term "Big brother is watching you" syndrome. Quite rightly citizens are afraid that their data on various files may be misused.

Selection of projects:

Even in advanced country there is criticism on the amount of money sent on projects at the cost of development of computer based projects for example in Medicine. Citizens are getting more concerned on this aspect.

Evil effects:

There is criticism about introducing computers at schools or fond parents buying computers for their children. The feeling is that the child tends to neglect studies, equally, the absence of remembering tables, they take easy way out using the computer even for simple additions. This is one view offset by the contrary view that it leaves the child time to learn more useful things.

The after effects of working on the terminal is still to be fully investigated.

A last word:

The computer is a gift of the twentieth century. It can be used destructively or constructively.

A socially desirable attitude in selections of projects is a desirable thing.

Emerging applications of information systems

It is said that the greatest rate of obsolescence is in the field of electronics. A thinker has said that were such strides made in the automobile field, we should have a car sold at ridiculous prices (like ten paisa) and it would give mind boggling performance (like a thousand km. per litre of petrol). The field of computers is a sub-set except that apart from the electronics, the juxtaposition of its components (in the form of an architecture); the driving force is software, giving scope for not only obsolescence, but also the for power never before achievable. The very fact of rapid growth makes it difficult to forecast to any degree of accuracy.

Technology: Rapid strides are being made here:

— Integrated circuits are reaching limits set by the laws of physics;

— Memory devices are getting to terrabytes storage potential;

— for recording, for printing and so on, new techniques

like Laser and optical devices are giving greater speeds for peripherals;

Architecture: The juxtapositioning of devices and components to achieve throughputs show greater innovation; distributed computing, parallel processing etc. will make the dividing line between the current concepts of PCs to super computers hazy. As Dr. Seshagiri said in an address to the Computer Society of India, in the not too distant future, there will be only two families of computers; Super Computers and Microcomputers.

Reliability: In a lighter vein, it was said that when the early valve based computers worked for an hour there was cheering on the sidelines. Tomorrow, reliability, maintainability and availability would be essential ingredients to give NO down time and 100 per cent "up" time, a combination of the other development would contribute to that status; allied would be the need for communication linkage reliability through not only good channels but also through efficient re-routing, confidentiality etc.

Software: The efficiency of which has always lagged behind technology by decades. The trend will be a synergism of technology, architecture and software to give users the best environment.

Applications: Is what the user wants; menu driven user-friendly systems will proliferate making the user to make full use of computer power;

Internal user: Whose demands will be satisfied by free access.

Society: Obligations to and observance of external factors; there would be greater emphasis on privacy: for example through Governmental pressures, economic constraints with emphasis to : prevention of industrial espionage etc. Traditionally CBIS has been Technology driven. Tomorrow the emphasis should be not on whether or not the product will work but what kind of work it will is; the criterion should be not the ability to do something but the advisability of doing it; the concentration should not be on how something done but on what is done.

We can visualise the inclusion in the home, in addition to the power, water, gas, the telephone, and devices working on these, an *information* outlet. Also contingent is distributing it around the house and equally, provide control of home devices like temperature control and perhaps security with connections to the Police and Fire Services all through the use of computer power.

SOHO (Small Office Home Office):

The home office unit will be in a room of the occupant's choice and will be the hub. Other units could be:

— the household operation unit that would control appliances, temperature etc.;

— the master security unit (near the bedrooms possibly) controlling intrusion of fire/theft.

There would be facility, through communication lines, which may be integrated with the telephone or cable television or whatever, giving access to all kinds of Services including access to Data bases around the world.

The home Information unit would consist of, typically,

— a 2 metre plasma screen on the wall with excellent resolution, with windowing facility for more than one user to access;

— a powerful microcomputer;

— disk drives of small physical volume but capable of megabytes of storage,

— integration with the television channels

— access to libraries, sports, database of all types;

— electronic mail;

— variable security devices;

— ability to telecommute or carry out office work in the comfort of the home; there will be less traffic on the roads as a consequence:

A word on expert systems

We already have some systems claiming to be of this category. These are off shoots of Artificial Intelligence (AI) and parallel processing developments. These are termed Knowledge Based Systems (KBS).

The nucleus is a knowledge base which contains data as well as assertions about the data; assertions are in computer processible form which are stored by it and inferences gleaned after duly organising and processing.

One type of KBS is the Expert System that is designed to support a non-expert to arrive at decisions. MYCIN is one such in the medical field to help diagnose certain infectious diseases. Its success rate is said to be very high *vis-a-vis* a general practitioner.

The future is very bright and with processing powers increasing manifold, they may even learn by experience.

The fifth generation

The second, third and fourth generations of computers were mere technology upgrades, dramatically ushered in. It was the Japanese that postulated "a discontinuity in idea seem inevitable" and, with fanfare, announced plans for the next generation; the West was caught by surprise but were not very far behind in planning for studies.

The Japanese stated that western computer technology is stuck in a mire, trapped by;

— Von Neumann architecture;

— Vast operating systems;

— Dedication to third generation languages;

— Avoiding relational databases or rather slow in developing them

— huge customer investment in existing programs;

— Vested (financial) interests in avoiding as opposed to evolution change.

The aim of the fifth generation is to enable socially valuable functions being handled by the man-in-the-street. Means of representing and possessing knowledge is necessary so that the computer can appear intelligent and provide expertise far beyond the capability of the human brain for certain highly specialised areas. Pictures, speech and human language should be employed between the machine and its users.

On the route to that target is the evolution of KBS and expert system that we have briefly seen.

The Japanese target is to produce, by 2000, a KB machine that cam access upto 100 million data items (each of which will require a thousand bytes of storage) and 20,000 assertions (called rules). Initially, the KB machine will employ a separate inference machine for processing the assertions; the inference machine will be fused with the KB machine. It is said that the inference machine will be able to process 100 million to 1 billion logical inference per second. To a large extent the inference can be processed in parallel. A highly parallel architecture capitalising on the cost of future microprocessors will therefore be used. The control mechanisms and software for this will be complex and highly innovative says James Martin.

There is great potential for the citizen of the future; he/she will be able to interact directly with his own, as well as public, data bases for day to day work, recreation and education. He/she will be assured of a high degree of security. His/her privacy will be respected. The great unanswered question is "what will the citizens of tomorrow do with the leisure time that will be a plenty?"

10

DEVELOPING ORGANISATIONAL INFORMATION SYSTEMS

This chapter considers the development of organizational MIS. It is concerned with the process by which such systems are brought into existence. Development activities become increasingly complicated as we move from personal, to work group, to organizational MIS. One consequence of this is that the users' role changes; users take less of a leadership role and instead become clients of others' services. For organizational MIS, users generally become clients of the in-house MIS department.

First, we consider the challenges in the development of an organizational MIS, we consider the challenges in the development of an organizational MIS.

Such challenges can arise from within the system and from outside the system and also from the nature of MIS. Next we will discuss strategic planning for organizational MIS: you will learn several ways in which organizations plan and prioritize development projects. In the third section, we will discuss computer-aided systems engineering (CASE), Finally, the last section discusses the use of prototyping in organizational MIS.

Challenges in developing organi-zational information systems

Developing an organizational MIS involves considerably more challenge than does the development of personal and workgroup MIS. Some of the reasons for this arise from within the system to be developed and some arise from outside the new system; some, however, arise from the nature of the organizational systems themselves. We will address each group of challenges. To understand this discussion, however, first consider the needs for a new organizational system in a manufacturing organization.

Scott Orthodontics manufactures exceptionally high-quality orthodontic appliances for orthodontists, oral surgeons, and dentists. Over 90 percent of the orders that Scott receives are for custom, one-of-a-kind items. Depending on the item, if may require from two days to several weeks to process the order. On rare occasions, when the required raw materials are out of stock, it may take six to eight weeks to manufacture an item.

Scott's customers, the dental professionals, want to provide prompt and efficient service to their patients. When they order from Scott, they need to know how long it will be before their order will be processed, so that they can schedule their patients' visits. Further, if there are going to be extensive delays in the manufacturing of an item, they need to know this so they can reschedule their patients, order a different product, or order from another source.

When there are delays, the sales force bears the brunt of the customers' complaints. The salespeople need to know the status of an order, what problems exist, if any, and how long it will be until the order is shipped. Unfortunately, Scott's order-tracking system is informal and inadequate. There is no single point of contact for salespeople to call. Consequently, salespeople often are forced to call production supervisors who, if sufficiently charmed or bludgeoned by the salespeople, will track down an order. The current situation is unacceptable to all, and as a consequence, Scott has decided to develop an order-tracking information system.

The flow of order processing

The entities involved in Scott Orthodontics order processing are shown in figure 1. Although this diagram uses dataflow diagram symbols, this is not a dataflow diagram. Instead, it shows the flow of an order. An order is received by sales and submitted to Order Processing where the customer's credit is verified and the order is validated for accuracy. The approved order is then sent to Manufacturing where it is produced. Raw materials are received from suppliers to produce an order. Finally, the order is transferred to shipping, where it is sent to the customer.

At a point in time, an order can be in any one of these processes, or it can be in transit between any two of them. When there is a delay with an order, the salespeople need to know not only where an order is in this process, but also how long it will be until the order is received by the customer. Knowing that the order is in Manufacturing is of little value if it will be six weeks until a required raw material is received.

Although there is no order-tacking information system, there are other information systems. There is a revenue generation system that includes sales, Order Processing, and Accounts Receivable. There are information systems in Manufacturing that are used to plan production and purchasing activity and to schedule people and machines. There are information systems in Purchasing and there is a general ledger system in Accounting. All of these systems are effective in accomplishing their function, but none of them provides information about the status and shipping date of a particular order.

Challenges to development from within the system

One purpose of an organizational information system is to integrate the activities of different departments into a single business system that produces coordinated, consistent responses to its Environment. To do this, the information system must bring together a diverse group of people, policies, procedures, goals, and expectations. This diversity creates a number of challenges to the development activity.

First, different departments will maintain different views of shared data. Further, Departments will vary in the ways in which they need to process data. Sales can delete an undesired customer record from the data sooner than Accounts Receivable can. Also, some departments will need to enter data that is only used by a different department. In this case, the quality of the data will suffer.

Allied with the differing views of data is the fact that users will employ the same terms to mean different things. A shipping date to manufacturing may be the date the order is completed. To Shipping, such a date is the date that it is delivered to the carrier. To Sales, it may be the date the shipment is received by the customer. Until the inconsistencies are known and understood, they will confuse the development activity.

Additionally, each department has its own goals and

expectations. For example, at Scott Orthodontics, personnel in Order Processing are evaluated on the basis of the number of orders they process; personnel in Manufacturing, on the other hand, are evaluated on the quality of their product. As a result, characteristics of the new system that enable orders to be processed more quickly will be applauded by order Processing: They may, in fact, be resisted by Manufacturing.

Departments will also have different goals and expectations regarding the type of system to be developed. Order Processing may want a system that is, in its basic character, a TPS. Manufacturing, on the other hand, may want a system for production supervision that is primarily an MIS. Shipping may want a system that primarily addresses product delivery, While Sales may want a system that improves product quality (Where the product includes sales support).

Another complication is that, very often, there are major differences in the competencies of departments. Manufacturing quality was of great concern to Scott's founder. Consequently, Manufacturing is full of well paid, hard-working, ambitions, capable. On the other hand, Order Processing was an afterthought. Hiring was done with less care, salaries are lower, promotions have been infrequent: as a result, the level of competency is lower. When the system development team convenes meetings among Order processing and Manufacturing personnel, This difference may become a problem. For example, Manufacturing may so overwhelm the discussion that Order Processing's needs may never become apparent.

Yet another complicating factor is that the departments compete with one another for dollars, management time, promotions, salary increases, and other resources. While it is all very good to state that the new system is to be created for the greater glory of all, when the system places one department in an advantage with respect to another, problems will result. Furthermore, it is possible for one group to gain control over the development activity and tern the project into an internal competitive weapon. Markus states.

> Designers have been known to build systems to change the balance of power among departments or other units in the organization. Because this design intention is not viewed as legitimate in most organizations, systems designed to increase one party's power and control over others are frequently masked in the language and appearances of improved efficiency or decision-making performance.

While such manipulation is undoubtedly rare, elements of it, or threats of it, do complicate the development activity.

Finally, systems often change the flow of work and the interactions among personnel both within and across departments. As this occurs, the Organization will change. Such change, however, is normally perceived as threatening and is resisted. The organizational change does not even have to be real; if the system is perceived as changing the organization, it may well be resisted. Impact of such resistance is great because it is seldom openly stated.

Challenges to development outside the system

Other factors that complicate development arise from sources outside of the boundaries of the system. These factors are listed. To begin, every information system resides in an environment of other information systems.

In the case of Scott Orthodontics, the new order-tracking system will reside amidst existing revenue generation systems, manufacturing systems, purchasing systems, general ledger systems, and others.

The development activity of a new system must take cognizance of existing systems. If the new system will obtain data from or send data to an existing system, then this need will form part of the new system's requirements. In many cases, this is no problem. In others, however, the interface will be awkward. Consider an example from Scott. The goal of the new system is to track customer orders. To do this, the new system could utilize data that is processed by the existing manufacturing scheduling system. That system, however, keeps track of production work orders, which are very different from customer orders. Thus, for the new system to use data from the existing manufacturing systems, some type of data conversion must be done.

Another complicating factor is that the new system may require more data from existing systems than they can provide. At Scott, it may be that the order-tracking information system will be able to obtain 90 percent of the manufacturing data that it needs from the current manufacturing systems. Obtaining the other 10 percent, however, may require a substantial change to those systems.

When this situation arises, the development team has a choice of three undesirable alternatives. They can develop an incomplete system, they can wait for the manufacturing system to be changed in the necessary way, or they can duplicate the functionality that properly belongs in a manufacturing system. All of these alternatives involve an unwanted compromise.

There are other external sources of complication besides existing systems. One is that the new project will compete for both dollars and development personnel with other systems development projects. Sometimes the development team is forced to compromise and cut back on necessary system capabilities because of a lack of money or time. The users whose requirements are unmet will be dissatisfied; their dissatisfaction will then pose another problem to be solved. The organizational prioritization of information system projects is an important issue and will be discussed later in this chapter.

Another problem is organizational politics. The new system may alter the organization external to the system as well as the organization internal to it. Or, the new system may give certain departments more power, more competency, more time, or some other resource. This change may be viewed jealously by departments that do not benefit from the new system's capabilities.

Sometimes, too, there is conflict between the user's needs and those of the MIS department. The MIS department may believe that it requires control over processing that the users do not want to give. For example, sometimes users want to make changes to organizational data on their own computers. The MIS department may prohibit this. The reasons may be valid, such as limiting the processing of partitioned, replicated data bases, as discussed in the previous chapter. Their reasons may also be suspect, such as a concern for loss of budget, personnel, or priority with management.

Challenges from the nature of large systems

In addition to challenges that arise from within the new system and from outside the new system, there are other challenges that have to do with the very nature of organizational systems.

First, organizational information systems are often far more complex than personal and workgroup systems. Complexity in this sense means more functionality against more types of data. Whereas workgroup systems provide functions needed by the workgroup, an organizational system provides functions needed by many departments. Furthermore, the data to be processed is often more complicated.

Second, organizational information systems are larger. There are more concurrent users, there is more data input and stored, and there are more reports and output produced. Although size does not directly impact the design activity, size does impact the amount of activity required for requirements definition and implementation.

Another complicating factor is that organizational systems integrate departments whose underlying activities may be inconsistent or incompatible. For the order-tracking system, It might be that Order processing has been blaming certain delays on Production for years, and that manufacturing has been blaming other delays on Order Processing for years. To substantiate these claims, Order Processing and Manufacturing may have set up independent business reporting systems. The new order-tracking system may bring these incompatibilities to light.

Organizational information systems often require considerably more work and longer periods of time to be developed than do personal or workgroup systems. The increased complexity and size means that more time must be spent in all five stages of development.

There are two consequences of this fact. First, to shorten the development time, organizations sometimes increase the size of the development staff. Unfortunately, there are diminishing returns on the addition of people to development projects. In short, the more people there are, the more human interfaces must be maintained, and the more time must be spent on communication and coordination. Larger projects are harder to manage.

Second, the problem with long projects is not just the delay that occurs before the system's benefits are realized. Another problem of lengthy projects is that, while development is underway, the business will change and the needs for the new system will also change. For a long project, it often occurs that, by the time the system has been developed, it is out of date. The organization must respond to market needs, new laws, and changes in ownership and management; as it responds to these things, the original requirements may be invalidated.

Finally, because of the increased complexity, size, and time required for organizational information systems development, it is more difficult for the development team and for any one individual to have an overall understanding of the system. In a classic book, Fred Brooks, one of the pioneers in large hardware systems development, discusses the importance for a single individual to have a vision for the conceptual integrity of the entire system. Without such vision, the system is vulnerable to inconsistencies, errors, omissions, and general ugliness. The larger the system becomes, the more difficult it is for anyone to have such vision. Additionally, the longer the project takes, the more likely it is that key personnel will be transferred or change jobs.

Organizational information systems planning

As stated, the development of an organizational information system is far more difficult than the development of a personal of workgroup system. Consider a construction analogy. Building a personal information system is like constructing a single-family house; building a workgroup system is like constructing a small office building; building an organizational system is like constructing a skyscraper. To build a skyscraper, much more planning and organization is required than for building houses or small office buildings.

Furthermore, the new system will reside amidst existing information systems, and it will compete with other project for resources. In terms of the construction analogy, he new skyscraper will need to be compatible with existing buildings; and it will compete with other skyscrapers that are being constructed or planned.

Business organizations need a family of organizational information systems that enable them to accomplish their business goals and objectives. They need a city of skyscrapers. At any one point in time, a number of different groups will propose the construction of a number of different systems. All of these proposed systems may be equally critical; some may be more critical than others; some may not be critical at all. There may even be other systems not being proposed that are more critical than those being proposed. To deal with this problem, the organization must have some means of planning and prioritizing projects. First, however, we will discuss the role of the MIS steering committee.

The MIS Steering Committee

Every organization has some means for setting priorities among information systems development projects.

Initially, as organizations first develop information systems, that means is simply a de factor system involving an informal committee. Perhaps the MIS director meets with the CEO and one or two other senior officers before making important or large dollar decisions. Such a de factor system is not generally effective in the long run, except for small organizations. As the organization develops more and more information systems. The planning issues become more involved. And it becomes apparent that a formalized forum for such decisions is needed.

To meet this need, most organizations establish a formal group that sets priorities for information systems development projects. This group, called the MIS steering committee, or some similar name, consists of senior level managers or executives from all of the organization's major departments.

First, the MIS steering committee has the responsibility for setting priorities among information systems projects. As stated, most often a number of different projects compete for the same dollars and human resources. The MIS steering committee resolves such conflicts. The committee may also take a proactive role in suggesting systems that should be developed or in approving planning projects whose goal is to determine which projects should be developed.

Another function of the MIS steering committee is to approve project plans, schedules, and budgets. Along with this, the committee often has responsibility for reviewing progress at major milestones in large or important projects and in giving "go" or "no-go" decisions for initiation of the next project stage.

The MIS steering committee also can have responsibility for approving the acquisition of hardware and/or major programs. Sometimes organizations establish a budgetary limit for the MIS director; if the cost of an acquisition exceeds that limit, then the committee's approval is required. Similarly, the committee can also be involved in the selection and hiring of key MIS department personnel.

Additionally, the MIS steering committee often sets high-level policy and standards. For example, the committee might establish the policy that users can buy only certain types of personal computer hardware or programs. Or, the committee might stipulate that the MIS department is to determine lists of approved hardware and programs from which suers must select. Finally, the MIS steering committee provides advice and assistance to the CEO, the board of directors, and other senior executives on an as-needed basis.

There are two general categories of information systems planning: top-down and bottom-up. Top-down planning starts with an analysis of the overall business objectives and works down to specific systems. Bottom-up planning starts with the needs of a particular system, develops the needs for that system and other systems on the same level, and works upward toward an integration of systems.

To understand the differences between these two, suppose that Scott Orthodontics sets out, without any further planning, to build the order-tracking system. If they do this, they are following a bottom-up strategy.

Now suppose that, in the development of requirements for the order-tracking system, it becomes clear that many information systems need work. Suppose manufacturing systems are totally inadequate, not only for the needs of order tracking, but also for manufacturing in general. Then suppose that the team learns that the order-processing system needs substantial rework as well. As the order-tracking system development progresses, it may turn out that the order-tracking system development progresses, it may turn out that the order-tracking system development progresses, it may turn out that the order-tracking system cannot be completed without an entire revamping of Scott's information systems.

To revamp so many of their systems, Scott will most likely use a top-down strategy. They will review the general business objectives and translate those objectives into the need for specific Then they will prioritize the development of those systems and set to work. The advantage of top-down strategies is that systems will be developed with an overall perspective of the needs of the business. Correct and appropriate systems will be developed on a timely basis. The disadvantage is that substantial lead time will be required to perform the top-level studies. This results in substantial delays before the first system is developed. Further, because of the lengthy time required, the business needs may change before the first system is developed. When this occurs, there is a danger that the top-level analysis will never be finished, a situation that is sometimes not so humorously referred to as analysis paralysis.

The advantage of bottom-up strategies is that specific systems are developed more quickly. The disadvantages are that the wrong system may be developed, that incomplete and ineffective systems may be developed, or that the system that is developed may have a short lifetime because it fulfills only a short-term need.

Critical success factor planning

A critical success factor (CSF) is an operational goal that must be attained to achieve success. Individuals, departments, and organizations all have CSFs. For example, a salesperson may believe that it is critical for her to identify at least two new leads per day, or an inventory manager may believe that it is critical to turn the inventory at least six times per year. CSFs are used in information systems planning to identify information needs, to identify types of information systems, and, ultimately, to identify requirements for information systems.

The underlying assumption in CSF-based information systems planning is that systems must exist that provide the information necessary to help management achieve the CSFs. If they do not exist, they must be created. The first step is to interview managers and to define the CSFs. Then the individual CSFs are combined into departmental and organizational CSFs. Finally, the CSFs. Finally, the CSFs are analyzed to determine which information systems need to be added and which of the existing systems need to be changed.

Usually all top-level many midlevel managers are interviewed and asked to specify personal and departmental CSFs. For example, the manager of Customer Support at legacy Systems believes it is critical for his to call three dissatisfied customers per day. That is one of his personal CSFs; typically, a manager will have several or many. At the departmental level, this manager may believe it is critical for the Customer Support staff to keep a customer on hold an average of less than 30 seconds and in no case longer than 3 minutes. Senior mangers are also asked to specify organizational CSFs. Examples of their CSFs are that should exceed 20 percent of sales.

Once all of the managers have been interviewed, the CSFs are combined. Herien lies one of the problems of this method. There is no clear-cut, well-delineated algorithm for combining CSFs. Four individuals in Customer Support may specify 10 different CSFs. Using this method, somehow these 10 CSFs must be combined into 2 or 3 CSFs. Similarly, five different organizational officers may specify a large number of organizational CSFs, which also must be combined into a few.

One advantage of the CSF method is that, by identifying the most important information needs, it focuses the planning and development of information systems on the highest-priority issues. It is broad in scope and thus unlikely to leave important information needs unaddressed. It is also simple and intuitive to understand.

The disadvantage are that the CSF method is time-consuming to perform, that the process of combining the CSFs is difficult and sometimes ambiguous, and that the result is no better than the ability of people to specify the CSFs. Also, this method focuses primarily on high-level managers. While such managers may be able to specify good CSFs at their level, they may not know and understand how the company truly functions at lower levels. Thus, the information needs of lower-level personnel may remain unaddressed. This disadvantage is compounded because the CSF method is not concerned with the details that must be specified to develop operational TPS systems. Because of these disadvantages, the CSF methodology is more likely to facilitate the development of MIS and ESS systems.

Enterprise analysis

Enterprise analysis, or, as it is also known, business systems planning, is a second top-down method for planning information systems. Whereas the CSF method is primarily concerned with generalized objectives, enterprise analysis is concerned with details-with identifying and correlating groups, their processing, and their data use. The CSF method asks each manager to consolidate his or her understanding into a few objectives. Enterprise analysis asks the managers for details about processes and data use; then the myriad details are combined, often with the assistance of computer processing, to identify which information systems are needed and what functions those systems should have. Enterprise analysis was invented by IBM personnel under the name Business systems planning.

Enterprise analysis is concerned with processes, organizations, data classes, and logical application groups. A process is an activity performed in dataflow diagrams. An organization is a group within the overall organization; usually organizations are formal groups and have names like department, office, and group. A data class is a group of data items that are created, changed, deleted, or used by one or more processes. A logical application group is a group of processes and organization that utilize the same data.

The first step in enterprise analysis is to select a group of managers who represent all the important activities of the organization. Then this group is interviewed to determine what processes they or their organization performs and what data is involved in those processes. The result of these interviews is recorded in a number of different matrices and other documents.

A logical application group associates processes and data classes. Using the process/organization matrix, process can be related to organizations. Thus, the result of an enterprise analysis is a set of logical application groups with the data classes, processes, and organization units for each. This set of groups can then be used to plan the development of information systems to support each application group.

Most logical application groups are applications within one of the seven major organizational functions defined. They identify specific systems that need to be developed within these functions. Usually, to a logical application group will involve a mixture of systems types. Often a single logical application group will indicate a need for TPS, MIS, and ESS within that group. Another way of saying this is that a logical application group serves all five of the basic business functions on the why face of the MIS cube.

The major advantage of enterprise analysis is that it provides a comprehensive review of the information requirements across the organization. It documents the use of data for all major processes and organizations. It is particularly useful for large organizations that require a thorough review of their processing and information needs. For example, the Social Security Administration used enterprise analysis in documenting its information requirements when revamping its information systems.

There are three major disadvantages of enterprise analysis. First, as with CSF, only managers are interviewed. Critical information needs of workers and first-line managers are interviewed. Critical information needs of workers and first-line mangers can be missed. Second, enterprise analysis is a time-consuming and expensive process. The Social Security Administration scheduled 10 years for their systems modernization plan. It began in 1982 and is scheduled for completion in 1992. Finally, enterprise analysis documents what is and not necessarily what ought to be. The results of an enterprise analysis are a set of logical application groups that are required to facilitate the existing processes, data needs, and organizations. Enterprise analysis does not suggest better ways of organizing business activity and dataflow.

Evolutionary planning

Whereas CSF and enterprise analysis are top-down methods, evolutionary planning works from the bottom, up. With this approach, the need for information systems and their requirements are allowed to evolve as the business evolves. This does not mean that development is unplanned or uncontrolled. Rather, it means that projects are proposed as the need for them becomes apparent. The proposals are periodically reviewed by the MIS steering committee and prioritized against projects underway and projects scheduled to be started. Newly proposed projects may preempt existing projects, or they may supplant projects that were about to be started.

The advantage of evolutionary planning is that projects can be started with a minimum of study time and expense. The intuitive judgment of the MIS steering committee members replaces the lengthy analyses performed using CSF or enterprise analysis. Furthermore, evolutionary planning is adaptive. Priorities for projects change as the business needs change. New system development projects can be started without having to reconsider or repeat portions of an extensive planning process.

The disadvantage of this approach is that it can result in a hodgepodge of systems that have clumsy and ill-fitting interfaces. It can result in a number of separate systems in search of a centralized theme. Furthermore, it places a great burden on the judgment of the members of the MIS steering committee. While these people may be wise and experienced, with the evolutionary planning process, they may not have enough data on which to base good decisions. Also, the MIS steering committee typically is a consensus-oriented, group decision-making body. Such groups can be dominated by one or two powerful individuals. If this occurs, the information needs of certain groups may receive undue attention.

Finally, evolutionary planning can cause systems development to proceed in fits and starts. It may be that, of three systems-say, systems A. B, and C- system C is the most important. If, at one point, the MIS steering committee is only aware of system A, then they will approve the initiation of this project. If, later on, the committee learns about system B, they will probably decide to place system A on lower priority and then start system B. When, finally, the committee becomes aware of the need for system C, it may decide to place system B on a lower priority and start system C. At this point, the management and staff of the MIS department may begin to lose confidence in the directions they are receiving.

Realize that evolutionary planning is not an unplanned or ad hoc approach. There is a plan, but it is a plan based on the needs that have been discovered, without an active attempt to determine what other needs may exist. A truly ad hoc approach would allow projects to be started as they are proposed to the MIS department, as long as the money holds out and with little intervention or prioritizing.

Proponents of the top-down approaches argue that they are superior because the business needs an overall strategic systems implementation plan to avoid incomplete and duplicative systems and costly rework. Proponents of the evolutionary or other bottom-up approach argue that they can build several incorrect systems for the time and cost that must be invested in top-down plans. Even if the systems are ineffective and incomplete, the process of building them will reveal more true requirements than will ever be identified by a strategic study.

Sometimes businesses elect to follow a hybrid approach. For example, the MIS steering committee might request a quick top-down overview of needs using either CSF planning or enterprise analysis. Given the results of this review, they would then follow evolutionary planning.

CASE

CASE is an acronym that has two meaning. Sometimes it stands for computer-aided software engineering, and other times it stands for computerised systems engineering. In this text, we will use the acronym CASE to stand for the latter meaning. It will refer to the process of using information systems to build information systems.

CASE technology developed as information systems professionals sought ways to use computer technology to improve their own productivity. Some professionals found it ironic that there were so many people in the computer field attempting to increase others' productivity but ignoring the computer's potential for improving their own.

While many of the ideas that form the foundation of CASE have existed for quite some time, it was not until the advent of the microcomputer that CASE technology began to see widespread use. Today there are dozens of case technology began to see widespread use. Today there are dozens of CASE products; almost every major corporation is experimenting with, if not operationally using, CASE products and methodology.

CASE, however, is more than a set of computer programs. CASE is an information system that includes all five components. There is CASE hardware, and there are CASE programs: these are sometimes called CASE tools. But, as CASE is used to develop systems, CASE database of system descriptors and other system parameters are also developed. Further, there are CASE procedures, which are sometimes called the CASE methodology. Finally, CASE requires a staff of CASE-trained systems development personnel.

It is a mistake to think of CASE as a set of programs. Technology without methodology is a waste of money. Organizations that have acquired CASE programs without changing their methodology have found little benefit from the too.

We will now survey the important components of CASE methodology and then discuss the capabilities of CASE tools.

Most significant applications of technology have come from the synergistic combination of existing elements. This is certainly true of computer-aided software engineering. Micro-computer-based analysis tools and mainframe database and code generators are coming together to address the entire software development life cycle. Artificial intelligence is the most recent technology to contribute to CASE.

The personal computer provided a break-through in software engineering by giving analysts the ability to generate high-resolution graphics, easily revise diagrams, and produce high-quality paper copies for delivery to users. While this constitutes significant automation of previous approaches, the use of local computer power to validate diagrams, enforce conventions, and capture information about processes took software engineering another step forward.

Developments in code generators progressed in parallel with those in micro-assisted design. Generators translate information combined from diagram, painted screens, and well structured descriptive text into code that can be compiled and executed. Early versions of these products did have shortcomings. Some generated only about 80 percent of a program's logic, leaving the additional 20 percent, usually the most difficult part, to be done by programmers, some produced code in a proprietary language or in a COBOL style barely decipherable by programmers. While the ultimate goal is to introduce changes by regenerating the application, maintainable code is good insurance until the technology matures, Finally, in some cases, the generated code required that the code generator be resident as the generated program runs, representing considerable resource overhead.

Recently, products have combined frontend analysis

and design tools with back-end code generators and central repositories for information describing the data entities and relationships uncovered in business analysis.

These repositories-a third-party DBMS or proprietary file structure-allow for the generation of more complete programs. The repositories also help enforce data naming standards and design methodologies. These application base management systems allow more or less seamless movement from graphics-based design to generation. The ease with which information captured by the design tools fulfills the code generator's input requirements depends on how well the vendor has integrated the front-and back-end components of its product....

Most of the progress in CASE has been directed at the process of building new applications. What of the massive investment in existing applications? Several restructuring tools convert existing code, usually COBOL, into structured code and create some documentation to make the structure evident....

Re-engineering of code is certain to require some fuel-based processing. More artificial-intelligence technology will find its way into CASE products in the near future. Knowledge of popular hardware and software environments and other information junior programmers are expected to know will be embedded in future CASE tools when they are shipped. Business policies, such as accounting and control standards and government regulations, might also be described to and then enforced by CASE tools.

In the near term, we can expect continued improvement in code generation, user interfaces, and consistency checking. It will still be necessary for a human operator to have a clear idea of what a system should do. The analyst will also continue to need the ability to communicate a large volume of information about a system and its environment to the CASE tool. In the long run, the continuing technological synergies tapped by CASE developers will result not only in higher productivity, but also in the redefinition of systems development.

While there is no single step-by step CASE methodology, there is general agreement about the stages and basic activities that need to take place for developing systems using CASE tools. This generally agreed-on process is a variation and extension of the five-stage process you studied.

Consider which summarizes this process. It begins with strategic systems planning, using one of the top-down methods. Enterprise analysis is frequently mentioned in CASE literature, though other methods are feasible. The result of the first stage is a set of specific systems to be developed. These systems may be submitted to the MIS steering committee for approval, and one of the goals of CASE tools is to provide documentation for that purpose. The remaining activities are repeated for each system to be developed. The development of two systems.

First, a systems analysis is performed. During this stage, requirements are developed, including dataflow diagrams and data dictionaries. This means that, with some CASE tools, requirements developed for one system can be used as input to others. This is useful when an office or department is common to both systems. In this situation, the dataflow diagrams and data dictionary that have been developed for one system can be used as a starting point for the analysis of a second. The next stage is database design. Here, the data dictionary data is used to develop a design of the database. Next, system design is undertaken. In CASE literature, the word system refers to the design of programs, user interfaces, forms, and reports. It does not generally include the design of hardware specifications, procedures, or job descriptions. The next stage is system construction. This term also refers just to the creation of programs, user interfaces, forms, and reports. Finally, the last stage is system management. During this phase the system is monitored, and changes are made to it in a controlled fashion. Versions of programs and other system components are managed so that configuration of the system is always known and under control.

Two activities underlie the development of the system. Process support refers to activities used to ease the development process and to ensure that it complies with the MIS department's development standards. It includes support for group communication, for creating, editing, and reviewing work, for provision of security and backup and recovery, and for compliance with quality assurance standards. Project management support refers to activities used to accomplish planning, scheduling and allocating resources, and controlling the development project.

The process described here is similar to the five-sage process you learned previously, but it emphasizes different aspects of the development effort. With organizational systems, much more time must be placed on the coordination of the new system with the existing systems. Also, since organizational systems are typically more complicated than personal or workgroup systems, this methodology places greater emphasis on design activities; and, since organizational systems are larger, the methodology places more emphasis on systems management.

This process, however, is not incompatible with the five development stages. The definition stage occurs during strategic systems planning; the requirements and evaluation stages occur during systems analysis, the design stage occurs during database and system design, and the implementation stage occurs during system construction and management. Again, this process is an extension and adjustment of the five stage development process.

The goal of CASE is to use computer technology to facilitate the development of information systems by automating or at least improving human productivity for each of the activities. The general architecture of a CASE product, which is a collection of CASE tools and a database of systems development data. The database, shared among all of the tools, is often called the CASE encyclopedia. The advantage of sharing the database is that the results from one stage of development are automatically available to tools in a subsequent stage of the process.

Not all CASE products have all of these tools, though most CASE vendors are developing a complete set, or are cross-licensing tools with other vendors to form a complete set. Not all CASE products have the same strengths. One product may have a particularly good systems analysis tools, while another product may have a particularly good database design tools. Consequently, some organizations mix and math tools from different products. They use a tool from one product for one stage and another tool for a different product or for another stage. Unfortunately, there is a problem with using multiple CASE Products: there is no standard structure for the encyclopedia. The data in an encyclopedia for one product may be incompatible with the data in an encyclopedia for another. Different products have different data standards. For example, one product restricts data element names to 10 characters; another product allows them to be up to 30 characters. Names from the second product cannot be input to the first. Organizations that plan on using several CASE tools must therefore restrict their encyclopedia data to the lowest common denominator.

There are dozens of CASE tools that facilitate the creation of dataflow diagrams. These tools are graphical and driven by mice. They provide a standard set of symbols that can be placed and moved about the screen, and they allow the input of both text and drawn art. Using them, dataflow diagrams can be developed with far greater ease and productivity than when drawn by hand. In addition, these tools provide automatic validation checking. For example, they ensure that, as a dataflow process is expanded to another level, no input or output is left out nor is any extraneous input or output added.

Analysis tools also provide capabilities for creating the data dictionary. Each dataflow, file, and process can be defined as described. These definitions are then carried forward into the design construction processes.

CASE products generally include a database design tool, although the capabilities very widely. Some such tools are simply graphical systems that aid humans in documenting a manually developed design. At the other end of the spectrum, some tools will construct a database design from data descriptions recorded in the CASE encyclopedia. Generally, there are problems with automatically generated designs, however, and such designs usually serve only as a starting point for human designers.

CASE products also include system design tools to facilitate the design of programs, menus, forms, and reports. By the time the system design tool is used, the data dictionary data and the database design will be stored in the CASE encyclopedia. The system design tools can access this data to make it easy for the human designer. For example, the user need only specify the name of a table when designing a report, and the system design tool can obtain the name of all columns of that table and guide the designer through the process of locating the columns on the form.

CASE products vary widely in their support for system construction. Some provide little, if any, support. Others provide tools that generate application program code, menus, and form and report descriptions. Many products produce large sections of source code that application programmers then move into the programs they write. This saves considerable time and eliminates the need for much of the programming work that is boring and repetitive.

There are also CASE tools to facilitate systems managements. Many of the tools are used for configuration control over programs and database structures. Changes are made to programs or to databse structures either to correct errors or to adapt the system to changes in system requirements. Either way, it is important to know what changes were made when, for what reason, and by whom.

Concerning process support, many CASE tools include word-and other text-processing programs, paint and draw programs, and a limited version of electronic mail. They also include facilities to control concurrent processing by development personnel and to protect the database against accidental, unauthorized, or criminal loses.

Finally, many CASE products include project management tools. These products include programs for developing plans and budgets, for scheduling system development tasks, and for allocating resources. These tools are used to organize and control the project and to report on progress to management and the MIS steering committee.

From this discussion, you can see that CASE is exactly what it sounds like. It is computer-aided systems engineering. CASE is not automated systems development. Instead, it is a methodology and a set of tools for developing systems with high productivity.

Prototyping

In its general sense, the word prototype means a sample, a pattern, an example, or the first thing of its kind. As applied to systems development, a prototype is a simulation, a demonstration, a piece of a system, or the first instance of a system. Usually prototypes are limited to hardware, programs, and data while there is no reason for prototypes not to involve the procedural and people components, they usually do not.

Prototypes are used for a number of reasons. For one, prototypes are used to demonstrate a concept or to sell or market an idea. It is often difficult for information systems professionals to indicate the benefits of a new system to management or end users from a description of product specifications. The prototype is constructed to show the benefits. Within an organization, prototypes are used to generate enthusiasm for a concept or to obtain financial or other resources. For example, start-up software companies prototypes to raise money for product development.

Another use of prototypes is to demonstrate the feasibility of an idea or an approach. Such prototypes are sometimes called proof-of-concept prototypes. Here, the essence of the idea is developed sufficiently in the prototype to demonstrate its technical feasibility. Such a demonstration might be required to show that the idea works at all, to show that it works with acceptable performance, or to show that it works within the constraints of a particular hardware configuration.

Another use of prototypes is to better understand requirements. users and professional systems developers come from two different cultures. Often, after an exchange of words, the two parties wonder whether or not they have understood one another. One way to check on the clarity of the communication is for the developers to build a sample of the entity being discussed, say, a report, and show that sample to the users. The users can then agree, or they can better describe what they want in the context of the prototype.

Yet another use of prototypes is to determine requirements. It may be that users and developers agree that they do not know what is required. One way to learn more about the need is to build a prototype and then apply it to the problem to be solved. The deficiencies of the prototype will then lead to more questions and further understanding of the requirements.

The reasons for building prototypes are summarized. The most common use of a prototype is to simulate the user interface. Prototypes are used to demonstrate the structure and processing of menus and other user commands. They are also built to represent data-entry forms. Often such prototypes simulate the user's action in processing the form. Users can employ the prototype in a sample situation and see how well it works.

Similarly, prototype reports are often constructed. Here, the users employ the report to perform whatever function they need to perform with it, and then they evaluate its effectiveness. From such firsthand experience, they can better comment on the appropriateness and usefulness of the form's design.

Another type of prototype is used to evaluate an algorithm, or processing method. Here the essence of the algorithm is programmed and tested, and sample data are submitted to it. Then the performance of the system is measured to determine technical feasibility. Performance is measured in terms of CPU cycles used, main memory required, disk accesses needed, and the like.

The last type of prototype we will consider is a prototype of an interface to another system. The new system may need to obtain data from or send data to another information system or even another computer. The only way to know for certain that the interface is as expected is to build a prototype and see. If data can be exchanged in the manner expected, then likelihood of surprises in the interface is greatly reduced.

There are a number of different types of prototypes. The simplest is a simulation, or slide show. This type is most often used for prototypes of user interfaces. With it, dummies of menus, data-entry forms, or reports are constructed. The user then uses the keyboard as he or she would with the actual system. Behind the scenes, a program reads files of canned screens and data to simulate what would happen with the actual system.

The advantage of simulated prototypes is that they are quick to develop. They also can provide a realistic feel of the character of the users interface. Usually, however, this type of prototype is restricted to a canned script or only minor variations from a canned script. This means that users cannot perform realistic tests against such a prototype.

When, as a business professional, you use or review a prototype, be certain to ask what type it is. If it is a simulation, or slide-show, prototype, keep in mind that none of the actual work in building the system has been done and that the prototype only indicates the nature of the idea. it does not indicate that the interface being demonstrated can actually be built.

A Second type of prototype was mentioned previously: it is the proof-of-concept prototype. Such prototypes are developed when there is substantial risk that the proposed design will not work. Building the prototype reduce the amount of dollars and other resources that must be placed at risk.

Proof-of-concept prototypes typically have a very rough user interface. Little time is spent developing program instructions to accept data or return results. Instead, the programming activity is focused on the particular aspect of the problem whose feasibility is unknown.

Most end users and managers are not qualified to

evaluate a proof-of-concept prototype. Instead, the prototype should be evaluated by competent information systems professionals who are disinterested in the results of the evaluation. Those whose idea is being tested are obviously not disinterested, nor are the opponents of the concept.

A third prototype is a partial-function prototype. Here a part of part of the actual system is developed and tested. Such prototypes are constructed to demonstrate a key feature of the system. Unlike simulation and proof-of-concept prototypes, the assumption behind a partial-function prototype is that the programs that are written will become part of the operational system. Thus, the programs, even though they only implement a part of a part of the system, are written with the same care and control as the operational system.

The advantage of such a prototype is that it need not be thrown away. The work invested in such a prototype saves work later. The disadvantage of such prototypes is that they are slower to develop and more expensive than either simulations or proof-of-concept prototypes.

The final type is pilot prototype. Here, all of a part of the operational system is developed. All of the features and functions, the user interface, the error processing, and the other aspects of some piece of the system are developed. As with partial-function prototypes, these prototype programs are assumed to become part of the system. Thus, the prototype is not thrown away. The advantage of such prototypes is that the user can truly test the system for adequacy. The disadvantage is that considerable time and expense are required to develop such a prototype.

Problems with prototyping

While there are substantial advantages of building a prototype there are also important disadvantages. First, the rapid development of a prototype may set an expectation in the users' minds that the system can be developed faster than it can. A complete system must not only process all of the features and functions, but it must also handle exception cases and errors. It may take more time to develop the program code for the latter items than it takes for the former.

Second, The prototype may gloss·over important issues. It may not reveal what later turns out to be the most critical and difficult to accomplish requirements. It may make the system appear to be easier to develop than it is and thus generate a false sense of optimism.

Third, Prototypes can lead to a false sense of how much has already been accomplished. Particularly with simulations and slide shows, if the reviewers do not understand that they are seeing a mock-up, they may believe that the technical challenges have already been overcome. They will later be surprised to learn that problems have been encountered in building something they thought already existed.

Although prototypes are described here for organizational MIS, they can be used for personal and workgroup MIS just as well. Prototypes for personal systems are usually simulations of user interfaces. They are developed quickly, often using form and report generators of personal DBMS products. Such prototypes are developed to understand and document requirements. They must be developed quickly because the cost of the system is too low to support extensive prototype development.

Prototypes for workgroup systems are more like those for organizational systems. All of the types of prototypes described here are used for workgroup systems.

The five-stage development process you learned also has a role in the development of organizational MIS. We have not focused on that method in this chapter, however, because you are already familiar with it. Do not conclude from its omission here, however, that the five-stage process cannot be used for the development of organizational systems. The five-stage process can follow any of the methods of strategic planning. The strategic plan indicates which systems need to be developed; once the needed systems are identified, the five-stage process can be used to develop them.

As described in the section on CASE, the standard CASE methodology differs only in emphasis and perspective from the five-stage process. CASE focuses on the development of programs and databases; the five-stage process focuses more on the development of all five components. Thus, if you use Case, much of what you learned about how to use the five-stage process to develop procedures and personnel components can be used to augment the CASE methods.

Finally, prototypes are easily combined with the five-stage process. A simulation, or slide-show, prototype can be used to help during problem definition and requirements definition stages. Partial-function and pilot prototypes can also be used for requirements analysis. Proof-of-concept prototypes can be used in feasibility assessment during the definition stage or to verify designs during the design stage.

CONTENTS